STEER YOUR CAREER

BY JOHN L. GAGNE

REVISED EDITION

Insights to a career in commercial trucking and bus driving from my 30 plus years of driving trucks and tour buses. Essential reading for those thinking about becoming a commercial driver.

Table of Contents

Introduction   07

CHAPTER 1 : Driving School   09

CHAPTER 2 : Choosing Your Ride   15

CHAPTER 3 : Specialized Commercial Driving Careers   19

CHAPTER 4 : Stories From The Road   42

CHAPTER 5 : Owner Operators   76

CHAPTER 6 : SAFETY FIRST   80

CHAPTER 7 : Drugs and Alcohol   85

CHAPTER 8 : Personal Privacy Concerns   89

CHAPTER 9 : Where's The Bathroom?   93

CHAPTER 10 : All Things considered   97

CHAPTER 11 : Body Mind and Spirit   104

Insights to a career in commercial trucking and bus driving from my 30 plus years of driving trucks and tour buses. Essential reading for those thinking about becoming a commercial driver.

INTRODUCTION

AAs a undisciplined young man in my late teens with no career goals, I decided to sign up for a metal fabrication course at a trade school. My father said often, "John, you need to do something with your life". My father, a carpenter by trade, hardworking, and a faithful Christian was right. I grew up with a good father and mother and was raised right. It must have pained them to see their son never try hard at school or show any ambition to self betterment.

 I was about doing what I wanted to do, like hunting, fishing, camping, and enjoying the great outdoors. The jobs I had as a young man consisted of cleaning large chicken barns, dish washing, and working at a shoe factory. My heart was never in it, and it was common for me after a while to hear the words, "your fired!

Well there I was, filling out papers to a trade school to learn metal fabrication and welding. You would have thought I should have known better, after all I was paying for this. But again, my heart wasn't in this either and I failed miserably, although I did learn how to weld which was a plus.

So there I was, living with my parents and it was time to find a job.

My bills consisted of room and board to my parents, a car payment, car insurance, and now a new bill, my student loan. At the time I didn't know it but this job was going to turn out to be a real blessing.

A plant not far from my parents house made laminates and chemical resins and needed a person to load and unload tankers of chemicals. This included moving the tankers around in the large yard and to a scale next door with a tractor.

Nowadays to get a job like this you would have to be an experienced CDL operator with a Hazmat endorsement even if you didn't leave the yard. I was hired with absolutely no experience driving a tractor trailer and was trained how to use the equipment and handle chemicals safely on the premises.

I was more interested in this job than my previous employment, and I took to it. The skills I learned at that job was a big help when I went to truck driving school.

Also the embarrassing failure that I had in metal fabrication school turned my thinking around. Before I even signed the papers for this new student loan for truck driving school, I was determined not to make the same mistake over again. And I didn't.

I was a model student and I aced the course. Soon thereafter I had my class A CDL with a hazardous endorsement, tanker endorsement, and a job with JB Hunt.

As you read this book, we'll start with my days in truck driving school and explore joys and challenges of a career on the road. We'll cover the pros and cons of the industry, essential safety practices, and tips for maintaining your physical, mental, and spiritual health while driving. I'll also share practical advice and some memorable experiences from my years behind the wheel. This book is a straightforward look at life in the driver's seat, offering insights that can only be gained from decades on the road.

1 DRIVING SCHOOL

Demand for commercial drivers is strong, making it a financially attractive career choice.

Do a search in your area for commercial driver training and see what they offer and what their schedule is and pick the one that works for you. Getting financial aid for the school that you want to go to should be easy, just talk to the school you're interested in and they can walk you through it.

Whether or not you want to drive a trailer truck or a bus, I would suggest if you can, get trained for both.

A class A CDL with the following endorsements, passenger, hazmat, doubles and triples, and tanker will give you plenty of options. Because if you're a bus driver and down the road you feel you want to go to tractor trailers, you'll have to take a separate road test and vice versa. The best bet is to get them all now. This will make you a more valuable driver and you'll have more choices. Your hazmat, doubles and triples, and tanker endorsements are obtained by just written tests.

 I started off with tractor trailers and then when I wanted to drive a bus I had to take more training and a separate road test.

 Alright, so let's discuss the cost of the training. In my case I had to get a student loan for my training. But today there are all kinds of opportunities for free training offered by companies looking for drivers. The way it works is, you train with them and agree to work for them for a certain time period and the training is free. Just do a search for the big trucking companies and call their toll free numbers and they'll have recruiters who will discuss all the details with you.

 If you go for this option you may have to travel to wherever the trucking company is and stay in a motel for the duration of the training. Also the time of the training varies, my training lasted eight weeks.

I want to give you some encouragement here, if you like driving and consider yourself a good driver, you can do this if you put your mind to it. It's not that hard. This is driving, not rocket science.

I want to give you some encouragement here, if you like driving and consider yourself a good driver, you can do this if you put your mind to it. It's not that hard. This is driving, not rocket science.

Your first time behind the wheel of a commercial vehicle may seem daunting but you'll quickly get used to it.

Also, if you have experience pulling a trailer, like a utility trailer, car trailer, boat trailer, or any trailer for that matter, and you can back it up okay, that's going to be a plus for you. Also you may be glad to hear, the longer the trailer is, the easier it is to back up.

 So here's how the training goes. You're going to have classroom time where you discuss all the laws of commercial driving, safety practices, and then all the potential questions that could be on your commercial driving written test. Towards the end of the course you'll have driver recruiters from different trucking companies coming to talk to you, and even to sign you up so you can work for them when you finish your training and get your license.

Then you'll have skills training with the equipment in a large parking lot, and then eventually on the road.

1) secure
2) check
3) call
4) don't
5)

NORTH
TRACTOR TRAILER SCHOOL
MANCHESTER N.H.

My experience in truck driving school went like this. The classroom time is where they gave you all the written material that you need, and the instructor went over everything with overhead projectors and really did a great job explaining everything in detail.

 All you really need to do is pay attention, take notes, be engaged, and ask questions when you need to.

I need to stress this point, you are not learning to become a doctor, there is only so much material that you need to learn.

I made sure that after the classroom time when I was back at my room, I reviewed my study material until I went to sleep. Also try to get good sleep so you'll be fresh and alert.

The people who taught in the classrooms were very good. When they were done going over the material we had tests and then we went over the material again. Repetition is the name of the game here and keywords that you hear over and over again. They went over every question that you may have when you do your written test, over and over again.

 I was very confident when I took my written test and the multiple choice questions were a breeze. I aced it!

So in my driver training they did the classroom time first and when that was over, they did the skills training in the yard with the trucks, and then eventually on the road with the instructors.

The skills instructors were excellent. They conducted training in a large parking lot equipped with multiple trucks and trailers, creating the perfect environment for hands on learning. The group was divided into smaller teams of three or four per truck, allowing for individualized attention. The instructor carefully demonstrated each maneuver, ensuring everyone understood the techniques, and we had ample time to practice on our own.

We started off with backing up in a straight line then we got into all kinds of backing maneuvers, like alley docks, ninety degree jack backs, parallel parking, and more. We also learned how to couple and uncouple the trailer, and preform proper pre and post trip inspections. We went over these maneuvers over and over again until we were very comfortable with them, then we went out on the road with the instructors.

I continued to try to get good sleep when I was back at my room. So when it was time to practice my maneuvers I was fresh and ready, and used all the time I had available to perform them.

When it was time to take my actual road test to get my CDL, it was a breeze, and I passed it the first shot.

However, there was people in the driving school who did not take it seriously. We had some people sleeping in the classroom because they didn't get enough sleep. They must have stayed up watching TV, or drinking or whatever, instead of sleeping when they got back to their room. And then I seen the same people in the yard fooling around instead of doing their maneuvers with the trucks. This behavior obviously didn't do well for them, but gave more time for the people who wanted to practice. So if you want this to work out for you don't be like those guys.

2 CHOOSING YOUR RIDE

Okay now it's time to choose your ride. Be assured that modern commercial vehicles are very comfortable to drive, with fully adjustable seats and climate control. With your new CDL and endorsements, you'll have plenty of options to choose from.

You need to keep in mind, that when you first get your license you need to start building experience. You could say, this is where the real learning begins, and this is true.

Companies would much rather hire a person with multiple years of driving experience, then someone who's fresh out of driving school. That being said, you'll still have many opportunities. I started my driving career with JB Hunt.

They didn't just put me in a truck and send me on my way. They put me with a driver trainer, and I was with him for several weeks. I learned a lot with my trainer, and it was nice to get out there to see other states and places that I never been before.

I remember being on the beltway around Washington DC for the first time and seeing all those Lanes of traffic. Also going into New York City was challenging, with lots of traffic, low bridges, and fast paced. I was glad to go there first with my trainer.

It's true that New York City scares a lot of commercial drivers, and they should be concerned, but even as chaotic as it is, people do learn how to go in there safely, and most companies pay more money for going into the city. I even talked to drivers who prefer to go there for one reason or the other.

My first time going into New York City was scary for me. I found the customer all right, but my heart rate was up, and I really didn't enjoy the experience. Think about it, you have a large vehicle that cannot be turned around easily, you have all kinds of unfamiliar streets, thick traffic, and low bridges, what's not to be scared of, right?

Fortunately, if you do work for a company, and they go to New York City, Brooklyn, Long Island, and the rest, you normally go to the same places. So if I went to a place that I had already been before, I was more at ease than going to a new place. Also, you can't always rely on your GPS. If you do get a GPS, make sure it's for trucking. You want to avoid low bridges and parkways, that are meant only for cars.

When I started driving a tour bus, my experience in New York City improved significantly. Typically, I'd pick up a tour guide upon arriving in the city. They'd hop on the bus, grab the microphone, and take charge, narrating every turn, road name, and the history of each landmark. All I had to do was listen and follow their directions, and everything flowed smoothly. It was perfect.

I was an over the road truck driver kris crossing the United States and sleeping in my truck. After about twelve years doing this it started getting old.

Fortunately, somebody with a class A CDL with endorsements and experience, has a lot of different opportunities to choose from. You can be a school bus driver, tour bus driver, local delivery driver, yard jockey, moving trailers around a large facility with multiple docks, local concrete delivery driver, and more.

When I got off the road, I got a job working as a local delivery driver. This was better for me now at my stage of life, I liked being home every night and sleeping in my own bed.

At first, I got into driving bus because the bus ministry at my church needed a driver.

Because I didn't have my passenger endorsement at that time, I had to study for the written exam, and take a road test in a bus. The written test for me was a piece of cake, and I used the church bus for the road test. Keep in mind that this passenger endorsement is not the same as a school bus endorsement, that's separate and I didn't get that.

 So now I was able to fill in when needed in the bus ministry, to bring people to church.

This also led to me getting a job as a tour bus driver. Being a tour bus driver, I did mostly short trips, but once in awhile I would do overnight trips as well.

In Maine, we have a lot of summer camps, and there are a lot of kids in those summer camps who need to be bussed to and from the camp, and to different events. There is also kids sports teams that need to go places for games. There are college sports teams that need to be bussed to and from their games. There are people that need to be bussed to and from cruise ships. There is elderly people who get together and take trips to sugar shacks, shopping, and sightseeing. There is people to be picked up and brought to airports, taken to trade shows, and other events. The list goes on and on, there is plenty of work for someone who wants to be a bus driver.

I liked it a lot because I like people. This is different than a truck, you have people, and many times you go to fun places like concerts and restaurants. You often get free food, and a nice motel with a pool, and even tips at times.

3 SPECIALIZED COMMERCIAL DRIVING CAREERS

Truck driving is often seen as a straightforward profession with long hours, big rigs, and endless miles on the road. But for those willing to pursue specialized training and take on unique challenges, the world of trucking offers a wealth of opportunities that go far beyond the standard delivery job. From transporting exotic sports cars to hauling hazardous materials, these specialized roles demand expertise, precision, and sometimes a bit of courage, but they also come with significant financial rewards.

What makes certain trucking jobs more lucrative than others? The answer often lies in the combination of risk, skill, and responsibility. Jobs that require specialized training, certifications, or equipment tend to pay more, as do those involving dangerous or high value cargo. These positions are not for everyone, but for those with the right mindset and determination, they can turn a trucking career into a highly profitable endeavor.

Let's dive into some of the most lucrative truck driving jobs and what it takes to get into them.

Hazardous materials (HazMat) trucking involves transporting substances like flammable liquids, corrosive chemicals, explosives, and radioactive materials. This work is inherently dangerous, as mishandling or accidents can result in environmental disasters or significant health risks.

Transporting hazardous chemicals and radioactive materials is one of the most specialized and high stakes responsibilities in the trucking industry. These materials are essential to industries ranging from energy production to medicine, but their transport requires precision, training, and the utmost care due to the risks involved. Among the most notable hazardous chemicals hauled by trucks are liquefied petroleum gas (LPG), anhydrous ammonia, and hydrochloric acid. LPG, widely used in heating, cooking, and fuel, is extremely flammable and can cause devastating explosions if mishandled. Anhydrous ammonia, essential for fertilizer production, is highly toxic and can cause severe respiratory damage if it leaks. Hydrochloric acid, a staple in the chemical manufacturing industry, is corrosive and poses risks to both human health and the environment if spilled. Drivers handling these substances must adhere to strict safety protocols, including regular inspections, the use of specialized tankers, and detailed route planning to avoid densely populated areas.

Radioactive materials represent an even higher level of risk and specialization. Trucks routinely transport medical isotopes, such as iodine-131 and technetium-99m, which are used in cancer treatments and diagnostic imaging. These substances are critical to modern medicine, but they must be transported under tight regulations to prevent contamination. On the industrial side, radioactive materials like uranium hexafluoride, used in nuclear fuel production, are shipped in reinforced containers designed to withstand severe impacts. Spent nuclear fuel, one of the most dangerous cargoes, is transported in heavily shielded casks to prevent radiation exposure. Even the logistics around such shipments are meticulously planned, involving coordination with local and federal authorities, as well as strict adherence to time schedules and security measures.

The risks associated with these materials are why drivers in this field are among the most highly trained in the industry. They must not only understand the properties and hazards of the substances they carry but also be prepared to respond to emergencies, such as leaks or accidents. For these reasons, hazardous materials and radioactive cargo transport is considered one of the most demanding, and lucrative sectors in trucking. The role these drivers play in keeping industries running smoothly and safely is a testament to their skill, dedication, and professionalism.

The increased danger and the need for specialized knowledge drive up the pay. HazMat drivers are often compensated well above the average trucker's salary because of the additional responsibility they bear.

Some jobs may require additional endorsements, like tanker endorsements for hauling liquid HazMat.

Employers often look for drivers with a clean driving record and experience in long haul or specialized trucking.

Hauling hazardous materials isn't just about driving, it's about understanding the cargo, following strict safety protocols, and being prepared to respond to emergencies. Drivers must also manage the stress of knowing that a single mistake could have catastrophic consequences.

Now let's look at oversized and overweight trucking. These loads include items that exceed standard legal dimensions or weight limits. This could range from massive construction equipment to prefabricated homes or wind turbine blades.

Oversized loads require extreme precision, coordination with pilot cars, and often special permits. Drivers must navigate complex routes, avoid low bridges, and manage challenging turns. The pay reflects the skill and patience required.

Some employers may require specific training for securing and hauling oversized cargo.

Be prepared to work irregular hours, as these loads are often moved at night or during off peak traffic times.

Drivers in this field must have an exceptional understanding of their truck's dimensions and handling, as well as local and state regulations for oversized loads. Patience and problem solving skills are critical, as every delivery presents unique challenges.

Transporting exotic cars is another specialized and prestigious sectors of vehicle transportation, catering to high end clientele who demand absolute precision and care. These vehicles include some of the most sought after names in the automotive world, such as Ferraris, Lamborghinis, Bugattis, McLarens, and Aston Martins. Beyond the well known brands, drivers might also handle ultra rare vehicles like Koenigsegg hypercars or Pagani Zondas, which are often produced in extremely limited quantities. Some of these cars are worth well over one million, with rarer models, such as the Bugatti Chiron Super Sport or the McLaren Speedtail, fetching upwards of three to four million. Classic and vintage vehicles, such as a 1962 Ferrari 250 GTO, which can sell for tens of millions at auction, are also commonly transported by drivers in this niche.

Exotic car transport requires more than just a standard car carrier. These vehicles are typically moved in enclosed trailers with climate control, hydraulic lifts, and advanced strapping systems to prevent even the slightest damage. Drivers must also have extensive experience and knowledge of the unique quirks of each vehicle, such as ground clearance and weight distribution, as many exotic cars are low to the ground or have sensitive suspension systems. Delivering these cars often involves traveling to exclusive events like car shows, private auctions, or directly to the homes of high net worth individuals.

The level of care required for these vehicles goes beyond the physical. The owners of such cars expect white glove service, complete discretion, and timely delivery. One misstep can result in significant financial losses or damage to a driver's reputation. With cars that cost as much as an entire home, or even more, the stakes couldn't be higher, but the rewards for mastering this specialized field can be equally significant.

The cargo is irreplaceable and often worth millions of dollars. The level of care and precision required, justifies the higher pay. Drivers must master the art of loading and securing vehicles without causing any damage. Knowledge of specialized equipment, such as enclosed trailers with hydraulic lifts is essential.

Driving tanker trucks is another option for the commercial driver. Tanker drivers transport liquids such as fuel, chemicals, or even food grade products like milk.

Liquid cargo is challenging to handle due to the "sloshing" effect, which can destabilize the truck if not managed properly. Tanker drivers must have excellent control and awareness, particularly during turns and stops.

Some employers may require HazMat certification, depending on the type of liquid being transported.

Tanker drivers need strong spatial awareness and the ability to adapt to the shifting weight of their cargo. This job requires a steady hand and a calm demeanor, as mistakes can be costly or dangerous.

Ice road trucking is another option for the commercial driver. Made famous by TV shows, ice road trucking involves hauling goods across frozen lakes and remote winter roads, often in Canada or Alaska.

The extreme conditions and short season mean drivers can earn in a few months what many make in a year. The risk of ice breaking or trucks sliding off the road justifies the higher pay.

Ice road trucking isn't for the faint of heart. It requires incredible focus, adaptability, and a willingness to face extreme cold and isolation.

Specialized trucking jobs aren't just about the money, they're about the challenge and the satisfaction of mastering a unique skill set. These roles often appeal to drivers who are looking for something beyond the routine of general freight hauling.

If you're considering moving into one of these fields, here's some things to keep in mind. Training is key, Invest in the necessary endorsements and certifications. Employers in these fields value expertise and proven capability. Build experience, many specialized jobs require years of experience in standard trucking roles. Stay Professional, a clean driving record and strong work ethic will set you apart.

The road to specialization isn't always easy, but for those willing to put in the work, it can lead to a highly rewarding career. Whether you're hauling hazardous chemicals, luxury cars, or oversized cargo, these jobs represent the pinnacle of trucking professionalism, and they prove that this industry has a place for those who aim high.

Now let's shift our attention to the world of specialized and lucrative bus driving.

When most people think about bus driving, they envision a city bus rattling along a crowded urban route, or perhaps a yellow school bus full of noisy children on the way to class. These are the images burned into the public imagination, and they are often accompanied by the assumption that bus driving is a simple repetitive job, with little variation or glamour. But like trucking, bus driving has a hidden world of specialized roles, jobs that go far beyond the mundane, offering not only higher pay but also unique experiences that most people can't even begin to imagine.

This world is filled with stories of drivers who transport famous people, high profile criminals, or operate under the watchful eye of the secret service. It's a world where the job requires precision, discretion, and a level of professionalism that separates the best from the rest. These jobs are as varied as the people who take them on, and they often come with fascinating challenges and rewards.

One of the most coveted roles in bus driving is working as a tour bus driver for famous musicians, actors, or other celebrities. This isn't just a job, it's a lifestyle. Drivers in this field don't simply ferry their passengers from one location to another, they become part of the entourage, responsible for the comfort, safety, and schedules of their high profile clients.

The pay for these positions can be excellent, but the demands are equally high. Imagine driving a luxury coach filled with expensive equipment and personal belongings, while your passengers rest, rehearse, or party in the back. You might be navigating through busy cities one day and remote backroads the next, always under pressure to be on time for a show or event.

The stakes are high, but so are the rewards. Drivers in this niche often find themselves in close proximity to famous people, sharing stories, meals, and even a laugh or two along the way. Of course, discretion is key, celebrity clients expect their privacy to be respected at all times. A driver who can maintain professionalism while keeping the wheels turning smoothly is worth their weight in gold.

When you think of the Secret Service, you likely picture agents in suits with earpieces, standing stoically near a political figure. What you might not realize is that the transportation of these high profile individuals often involves highly specialized bus drivers. Whether it's a campaign tour for a presidential candidate or moving dignitaries during a global summit, the drivers in these roles are part of a much larger security operation.

These jobs require more than just excellent driving skills. Drivers must undergo rigorous background checks, maintain impeccable records, and sometimes even complete security training. The buses themselves are often customized with advanced security features, from bulletproof glass to encrypted communication systems.

The challenges are immense. Routes must be meticulously planned, with contingency options for every possible scenario. Drivers must be prepared for sudden changes, detours, or even evacuation procedures. It's a high pressure role, but for those who thrive under stress and want to serve in a unique capacity, driving for the secret service can be an incredibly rewarding career.

These buses are designed with safety in mind, featuring reinforced windows, locked compartments, and limited access points. Drivers often work alongside armed guards, ensuring that every transfer is conducted with maximum caution.

The stakes are high in this field, not just because of the nature of the passengers but also because of the unpredictability of the job. A simple mechanical issue on the road can become a potential security threat. Yet for those who choose this line of work, there is a sense of purpose in ensuring that justice is served and society is kept safe.

It might sound surprising, but some school bus driving jobs fall into the lucrative category, especially when dealing with private schools or institutions catering to the wealthy. These roles often involve driving smaller, luxury buses outfitted with plush seats, advanced safety features, and high end amenities.

In these cases, the parents expect the absolute best for their children, and they are willing to pay a premium for it. The drivers must be reliable, professional, and personable, as they often interact directly with parents, teachers, and administrators. These jobs may not be as glamorous as driving a tour bus, but they offer stability, respect, and excellent pay for those who excel at customer service.

In the world of business, time is money. Corporate shuttle drivers transport executives, clients, and employees between offices, airports, and meetings. These buses are often high tech, featuring Wi-Fi, conference areas, and other amenities designed to keep passengers productive on the go.

The job demands punctuality, discretion, and adaptability. Drivers in this field often work irregular hours to accommodate their clients' demanding schedules. The pay reflects the responsibility, as these roles cater to high level professionals who expect seamless service.

For those who crave adventure, working as a tour bus driver in remote or exotic locations can be an incredibly rewarding experience. Imagine guiding a group of tourists through Alaska's rugged wilderness, along the twisting roads of the Swiss Alps, or across the sweeping plains of Africa.

These jobs combine the skills of a driver with the personality of a guide. Drivers often share their knowledge of local history, culture, and geography, adding an educational aspect to the journey. The pay can be excellent, especially for seasonal roles in high demand destinations.

However, these jobs aren't without challenges. Driving in remote areas often means dealing with unpredictable weather, limited infrastructure, and the responsibility of keeping passengers safe in unfamiliar terrain.

Breaking into these high paying roles often requires more than just a Commercial Driver's License (CDL). Experience is key, as most employers want to see a proven track record of reliability and professionalism. Networking also plays a significant role, many of these jobs are filled through referrals or insider connections.

Specialized training or endorsements may be required, particularly for roles involving security or hazardous conditions. Drivers should also be prepared to invest in continuous learning, whether it's mastering new technologies, understanding advanced safety protocols, or adapting to the unique demands of their passengers.

Ultimately, the best way to position yourself for a lucrative bus driving job is to build a reputation for excellence. Employers in these fields value drivers who are not only skilled but also adaptable, personable, and trustworthy.

The world of specialized bus driving offers opportunities that go far beyond the ordinary. These roles demand more skill, responsibility, and dedication than standard driving jobs, but they also come with unique rewards, both financial and personal. Whether you're chauffeuring celebrities, safeguarding dignitaries, or guiding tourists through breathtaking landscapes, these jobs offer a chance to turn a driving career into something truly extraordinary.

Enter the world of mobile labs and testing units. Commercial driving has long been associated with hauling freight, delivering goods, or transporting passengers. However, there's a specialized niche within the industry that combines logistics, innovation, and technical expertise. Mobile labs and testing units.

These vehicles are essentially self contained, state of the art facilities on wheels, designed to bring specialized services directly to communities, workplaces, or remote locations. For drivers and technicians operating these units, the job goes far beyond traditional driving, it's about precision, adaptability, and often serving critical roles in healthcare, research, and public safety.

One of the most common examples of mobile testing units is mobile medical labs. These vehicles are equipped with advanced medical technologies, such as CAT scan machines, MRI systems, or mammography equipment, allowing healthcare providers to deliver diagnostic services directly to patients who may not have access to hospitals or clinics. Mobile medical units are particularly valuable in rural areas, where healthcare facilities can be hours away. Driving these labs isn't just about navigating roads, it requires careful handling to ensure sensitive equipment remains stable and functional during transport. Drivers often receive specialized training to understand how to operate or maintain this equipment, adding a layer of technical expertise to their role.

Drug testing units are another growing sector in the mobile lab industry. Companies or organizations often use these units to perform on site drug and alcohol screenings, especially in industries like construction, trucking, and manufacturing, where safety is critical. These mobile labs are typically stationed at worksites, allowing for efficient and immediate testing without the need to send employees off site. For the drivers of these units, discretion and professionalism are essential, as they are often interacting directly with employees and employers in sensitive situations.

Mobile labs aren't limited to medical testing, they're also used extensively in scientific research and environmental testing. For example, some labs are designed to analyze water quality in real time, testing for pollutants in rivers, lakes, and municipal systems. Others are outfitted for soil analysis, used by agricultural organizations or construction companies to ensure land suitability for farming or building. These vehicles are often sent into disaster zones, or areas of environmental concern, to provide on the ground data that would otherwise take days or weeks to gather. Driving these units requires not only logistical skill, but also a deep understanding of the mission they serve.

One fascinating niche within the mobile lab world is mobile forensic labs. These units are used by law enforcement and crime scene investigators to process evidence in real time. Outfitted with tools for DNA analysis, toxicology tests, and fingerprinting, they allow investigators to expedite the processing of crucial evidence. For drivers, this means not only navigating to remote or urban crime scenes, but also understanding the importance of their role in maintaining the integrity of evidence during transport.

Mobile educational labs also play a unique role in underserved communities. These vehicles bring STEM, science, technology, engineering, and mathematics education to schools, complete with hands on experiments and demonstrations. Drivers of these units often double as facilitators, assisting teachers and students in engaging with the equipment. This adds a rewarding, interactive component to the job, where drivers see the direct impact of their work on young learners.

One area that's gaining attention in recent years is mobile veterinary clinics. These units bring essential services like spaying, neutering, vaccinations, and minor surgeries to rural or underserved areas. Designed to minimize stress for animals and their owners, these units are a lifeline for pet owners who may not otherwise have access to care. Drivers in this field often have a love for animals, as their role may involve assisting with handling and setting up equipment.

Mobile disaster response units represent another critical use of this technology. These vehicles are deployed during natural disasters, pandemics, or large scale emergencies to provide immediate support. Some are mobile command centers for coordinating emergency responses, while others serve as triage centers or even morgues. Drivers of these units are often part of specialized teams trained to handle high pressure situations, making their work both challenging and deeply impactful.

The world of mobile labs even extends to high tech industries like cybersecurity. Mobile data centers and IT recovery units are used to respond to cyberattacks or infrastructure failures. These vehicles are equipped with servers, data recovery systems, and advanced diagnostic tools, allowing companies to recover operations quickly in the event of a disaster. Drivers in this niche need to be technologically savvy and prepared to work alongside IT professionals.

Operating mobile labs and testing units comes with unique challenges. The vehicles are often larger than traditional commercial trucks, outfitted with sensitive and expensive equipment that requires careful handling. Routes must be planned meticulously to avoid rough roads or sharp turns that could damage the equipment. Additionally, drivers must often adhere to strict schedules, as delays could impact critical services like medical diagnostics or emergency response.

For those considering a career in this field, the rewards go beyond financial compensation. Drivers of mobile labs often report a sense of pride in knowing their work directly benefits communities, whether it's delivering life saving healthcare, protecting the environment, or aiding in disaster recovery. Many jobs in this niche require specialized training, but the added responsibility is balanced by the satisfaction of contributing to meaningful work.

The demand for mobile labs and testing units continues to grow as technology advances, and industries seek more efficient on site solutions. These vehicles represent the cutting edge of what commercial driving can achieve, merging the logistics of transportation with the expertise of specialized fields. For drivers looking to make an impact beyond moving goods, the world of mobile labs offers a unique and rewarding path that combines innovation, service, and a spirit of adventure.

One of the most fascinating and highly specialized niches in the trucking industry involves hauling equipment, parts, and payloads for the aerospace sector. This is a realm where logistics meets cutting edge technology, and every mile carries with it the weight of innovation, precision, and often a multi million dollar cargo. Transporting satellites, rocket components, and other aerospace materials requires not just expertise in commercial driving, but an understanding of the meticulous requirements that make these jobs some of the most demanding, and rewarding in the industry.

Imagine transporting a satellite worth hundreds of millions of dollars, destined to orbit Earth and facilitate communication, navigation, or even deep space exploration. Satellites are incredibly fragile, despite their high tech construction, and their journey from the manufacturing facility to the launch site is one of the most critical phases before liftoff. These cargos are housed in custom built containers designed to control temperature, humidity, and even vibrations. The trucks that haul them are no ordinary rigs, they are often equipped with advanced suspension systems to ensure the smoothest possible ride, and they're driven by operators who understand that even the smallest jolt could result in catastrophic damage.

One of the most prominent names in this field is SpaceX, Elon Musk's groundbreaking aerospace company that has revolutionized space travel. SpaceX frequently relies on specialized trucking companies to transport critical components like Falcon 9 rocket stages or the Dragon spacecraft. These components are massive, often exceeding standard height and width limits, which means obtaining special permits, using escort vehicles, and meticulously planning routes to avoid low overpasses, tight turns, or rough roads. Drivers in this field must have extensive experience with oversized loads and a keen attention to detail to ensure the equipment arrives without a scratch.

A particularly high stakes job involves transporting rocket engines, such as SpaceX's Merlin or Raptor engines, which are marvels of engineering. These engines are shipped in reinforced crates and monitored closely throughout the journey. Drivers may work alongside engineers or technicians who accompany the load to ensure everything remains secure. The level of trust and responsibility placed on the driver is unparalleled. After all, these engines represent not only an enormous financial investment, but also the hopes and ambitions of cutting edge space exploration.

Transporting full rocket stages presents its own challenges. These stages can be over one hundred and fifty feet long and weigh tens of thousands of pounds. For example, the Falcon 9's first stage must be transported in horizontal sections, requiring custom trailers with extendable platforms and precision steering capabilities. These trailers are often referred to as "dual lane trailers" because they can occupy two lanes of traffic, and they're escorted by pilot cars to ensure safe passage. The drivers tasked with these jobs are among the best in the business, combining technical expertise with an unflappable demeanor in the face of high pressure situations.

It's not just SpaceX that relies on specialized haulers. NASA, Boeing, Lockheed Martin, and other major aerospace players all depend on trucking to move their hardware. Consider the journey of a satellite built by Lockheed Martin in Colorado, destined for a launch pad at Cape Canaveral Florida. The trip involves thousands of miles and countless logistical challenges. In many cases, these satellites are transported in hermetically sealed containers aboard air ride trailers. The containers are equipped with shock absorbers, temperature controls, and vibration dampening systems to create a near laboratory environment on the road. Drivers in this niche often have to meet strict security protocols, undergoing background checks, and sometimes even obtaining security clearances due to the sensitive nature of their cargo.

The stakes are equally high when transporting components for the International Space Station (ISS).

These parts, ranging from solar panels to life support modules, are integral to the functioning of one of humanity's most ambitious projects. The precision required to manufacture these components extends to their transport, with every detail meticulously planned to avoid damage or delays. Drivers are often part of a larger team that includes logistics coordinators, engineers, and security personnel, all working together to ensure a seamless journey.

Another fascinating aspect of aerospace hauling is the need to move test hardware and prototypes. Before a rocket or spacecraft ever reaches the launch pad, it undergoes extensive testing. Some of this testing happens at specialized facilities, requiring the hardware to be transported under highly controlled conditions. These trips often involve "dry runs" to practice the logistics of moving the equipment before the actual hardware is loaded. The driver plays a crucial role in these rehearsals, working closely with the team to identify potential issues and fine tune the operation.

Perhaps one of the most challenging jobs in this field is transporting spaceflight hardware internationally. For example, parts manufactured in Europe might need to be transported to the United States for assembly. These jobs often involve multi modal transport, where trucking is just one part of the journey. The driver's role might include navigating to ports or airports, coordinating with customs officials, and ensuring the cargo is transferred seamlessly to ships or planes.

The lifestyle of a driver in the aerospace sector is as unique as the cargo they transport. These drivers often spend weeks preparing for a single trip, studying routes, attending safety briefings, and coordinating with multiple teams. Once on the road, they face long hours and intense scrutiny, as every move is monitored to ensure the cargo's safety. Yet for many, the sense of purpose and the knowledge that they're contributing to humanity's progress make it all worthwhile.

The world of aerospace hauling is not just a job, it's a front row seat to history. Whether delivering rocket stages to a launch site, transporting a satellite destined to orbit Mars, or carrying components for a spacecraft that will explore the outer reaches of our solar system, these drivers are an integral part of the story. Their work ensures that the dreams of engineers, scientists, and visionaries can take flight, one carefully planned mile at a time. For those with the skill, dedication, and love of the road, aerospace hauling represents the pinnacle of specialized commercial driving, a rare blend of technical precision and boundless ambition.

Now let's look at the animal transport niche. Transporting animals is one of the most challenging and fascinating niches in the world of commercial driving. It's not just about moving cargo from one location to another, these are living breathing beings, each with their own needs, behaviors, and quirks. Whether it's thoroughbred racehorses, cattle headed to market, or exotic animals destined for zoos, transporting animals requires specialized equipment, careful planning, and an acute understanding of the responsibility involved. The stakes are high, both for the animals welfare, and the financial investment often tied to them. Every load tells a story, and every trip is an exercise in patience, skill, and sometimes nerves of steel.

For drivers transporting livestock like cattle or pigs, the equipment is designed for efficiency and safety. Livestock trailers, often referred to as "cattle pots," are specifically built to ensure proper ventilation and prevent animals from slipping or injuring themselves during transit. These trailers are sturdy, with nonslip flooring and partitions to separate animals into groups to reduce stress and prevent overcrowding. Loading and unloading livestock is an art in itself. A well trained driver knows how to calmly guide animals up ramps and into pens, understanding that fear or confusion can quickly turn into chaos.

Transporting horses is an entirely different ballgame. These animals, often worth thousands or even millions of dollars, require a level of care that borders on luxury. Horse trailers come in various sizes, from small two horse bumper pull models, to massive tractor trailer rigs equipped with stalls, feeding areas, and even climate control. Some high end trailers are designed like mobile stables, complete with padded walls to prevent injuries and sophisticated suspension systems to minimize vibrations during transit. Drivers in this field often work closely with handlers or veterinarians to ensure the horses are calm and comfortable. A nervous horse can be dangerous, and a panicked one can cause significant damage to the trailer, or itself.

Zoo animals present yet another level of complexity. Transporting a tiger, elephant, or giraffe isn't as simple as loading them into a crate and hitting the road. Each species has unique requirements for space, climate, and feeding schedules. For instance, giraffes require custom built trailers with high roofs or open tops, while large predators like lions and bears need reinforced enclosures to ensure safety for both the animals and the driver. Many zoo animals are accompanied by handlers or zookeepers during transit, who monitor their health and behavior throughout the journey. These trips are meticulously planned, often involving coordination with multiple agencies to secure permits and ensure routes avoid unnecessary delays.

Stories from the road often highlight the unpredictability of transporting animals. One driver who specialized in moving exotic animals for circuses and zoos recalled a trip involving an elephant. The animal was calm during most of the journey but became agitated during a long delay at a weigh station. The driver and the handler worked together to soothe the elephant by spraying it with water and feeding it treats until they could get back on the road. The incident underscored the importance of adaptability and quick thinking when dealing with living cargo.

In another instance, a driver transporting racehorses shared the nerve wracking experience of hauling prized thoroughbreds to a major event. The horses were accompanied by their handlers, who constantly checked on them during the journey. One horse became restless, kicking the walls of its stall, which could have led to serious injury. The driver had to pull over and work with the handlers to calm the animal, highlighting the delicate balance of professionalism and empathy required in this line of work.

Cattle transporters often have their own set of challenges, particularly in extreme weather. Keeping animals cool in the heat or warm during a sudden cold snap is a constant concern. Many drivers recall long stretches of highway where they stopped frequently to check on the animals, ensuring they had adequate ventilation and water. These moments serve as reminders that transporting animals is not just a job, it's a responsibility to safeguard the lives entrusted to you.

Drivers in this field must also be prepared for the unexpected. Livestock can escape during loading or unloading, leading to chaotic situations. One driver told the story of a steer that managed to break free at a rest stop, leading to a two hour ordeal involving other truckers and local law enforcement to corral the animal. While these stories often end with a laugh, they're a testament to the unpredictability and challenges of transporting animals.

The legal and ethical considerations of animal transport add another layer of complexity. Drivers must comply with stringent regulations regarding the welfare of animals during transit. This includes adhering to limits on how long animals can be on the road without rest or water, as well as ensuring that trailers are cleaned and disinfected between loads to prevent the spread of disease. Violations can result in hefty fines, not to mention harm to the animals and the driver's reputation.

Transporting animals is more than just a specialized niche, it's a calling. It requires a unique blend of skills. The driving expertise to handle large, often unwieldy trailers, the emotional intelligence to read and respond to the needs of animals, and the problem solving abilities to adapt to the unexpected. For those who excel in this field, it's not just about the paycheck, it's about the satisfaction of knowing you've played a part in delivering something precious, whether it's livestock for a farmer, a champion horse for a trainer, or a rare species for a zoo. Every journey is a story, and every load is a reminder of the intricate connection between humanity and the animal world.

Specialized commercial driving would not be complete without mentioning one of the most colorful and challenging niches in the industry, transporting circuses and carnivals. This unique line of work isn't just about moving cargo, it's about moving a way of life. Drivers in this field don't simply haul equipment; they're an integral part of a traveling community, responsible for transporting everything from towering Ferris wheels and elaborate stages to exotic animals and entire temporary towns. The lifestyle is demanding, but for those who embrace it, it offers an unparalleled sense of adventure and camaraderie.

Transporting a circus or carnival requires specialized trailers designed for heavy, oversized, and often oddly shaped loads. A typical carnival ride for example, is far from a simple piece of machinery. It may involve massive rotating arms, hydraulic systems, and hundreds of individual parts that must be securely packed and carefully transported. Trailers for these loads are often custom built with extendable platforms, hydraulic lifts, and reinforced frames, to handle the unique requirements of carnival rides. Ferris wheels for instance, are disassembled into large sections and loaded onto flatbeds, while smaller rides may fit into enclosed trailers for added protection.

Drivers in this field must have experience with oversized loads, as they often transport equipment that exceeds standard height, width, or weight limits. Permits and route planning are critical, especially when navigating through urban areas or crossing under low clearance bridges. The stakes are high, not just because of the financial value of the equipment, but also because any delay or damage can disrupt the carefully orchestrated schedule of a traveling carnival or circus.

But it's not just about the rides. Circuses and carnivals are essentially mobile cities, complete with tents, concessions, living quarters, and even water and power systems. Drivers may haul massive canvas tents rolled into tight bundles, generators that power the entire operation, and kitchens that serve hundreds of people. Some drivers are tasked with transporting the personal trailers that serve as living spaces for performers and workers, adding an intimate connection to the people who call the road their home.

The human aspect of this lifestyle is as unique as the cargo. Drivers often become part of the tight knit community that defines circuses and carnivals. These aren't just coworkers, they're families, traveling together for months at a time, sharing meals, stories, and the challenges of life on the road. Drivers might find themselves setting up alongside acrobats, animal trainers, and concession workers, all working together to bring the magic of the show to life.

One driver who spent years hauling for a well known circus, described the lifestyle as "organized chaos." He recalled driving through the night to ensure the equipment arrived on time for a performance, only to turn around and help unload and assemble the stage. "You're not just a driver" he explained. "You're part of the crew. Everyone pitches in to make it happen."

The challenges of the job go beyond the logistics of transport. Weather is a constant concern, as rain or high winds can delay setup or damage equipment. Drivers must be prepared for the unexpected, from breakdowns on remote highways to navigating muddy fairgrounds after a storm. One memorable story involved a driver who got stuck in a field after delivering a carousel. The entire carnival crew came together, using a combination of tractors, planks, and sheer determination to free the truck and ensure the ride was ready for the opening night.

Transporting exotic animals adds another layer of complexity. While modern circuses have largely moved away from animal acts, some still require specialized trailers for transporting horses, dogs, or even camels. These trailers are equipped with ventilation systems, padded interiors, and feeding stations to ensure the animals' comfort and safety during transit. Drivers tasked with transporting animals often work closely with handlers, who accompany the cargo to monitor the animals' well being.

The lifestyle of a carnival or circus driver is as unique as the job itself. Unlike traditional long haul drivers, these individuals often spend extended periods at their destinations, living and working alongside the crew until it's time to pack up and move to the next location. This rhythm creates a sense of belonging that's rare in the trucking world. Drivers are part of the show's success, and there's a shared pride in seeing the crowds enjoy what they've helped bring to life.

For many drivers, the appeal of this work lies in its unpredictability and the chance to see the country in a way few others do. One day, you might be hauling a Tilt A Whirl through the desert, the next, you're navigating a bustling city to deliver a high wire rig. The scenery changes constantly, as does the sense of purpose that comes from being part of something larger than yourself.

The history of circus and carnival transport adds an extra layer of romance to the job. These traveling shows have been a part of cultural life for centuries, and the logistics of moving them have always been a marvel. From the days of horse drawn wagons to modern tractor trailers, the evolution of circus and carnival transport is a testament to human ingenuity and determination.

Today, the industry continues to evolve, with technology playing a bigger role in planning and logistics. GPS systems, automated routing software, and real time communication have made the job more efficient, but the spirit of the work remains unchanged. It's still about bringing joy and wonder to towns and cities across the country, one truckload at a time.

For those who thrive on challenge and adventure, transporting circuses and carnivals offers a unique blend of hard work, community, and a front row seat to one of the most enduring forms of entertainment. It's a job like no other, where the destination is as important as the journey, and every mile brings the magic of the show closer to the audience.

For those willing to go the extra mile, the road ahead is filled with possibilities. The question is, which path will you choose?

4 STORIES FROM THE ROAD

Back in the 1990s, Brownsville Texas was a vastly different place compared to the Brownsville of today amidst the ongoing border crisis. The small border town at the southernmost tip of Texas was characterized by a quieter more community driven way of life, with a strong emphasis on local culture, close knit neighborhoods, and bustling yet relatively peaceful cross border commerce. Unlike the heavily militarized and politically charged atmosphere of today, the border was more fluid, with residents frequently crossing into Matamoros for shopping, dining, and family visits without the heightened tensions or scrutiny of contemporary times. Back then, issues like human trafficking and large scale migrant caravans were not as visible, and federal immigration enforcement was less prominent in everyday life. Brownsville's economy was centered around agriculture, local businesses, and a growing emphasis on its ports, while its cultural identity was deeply rooted in the blending of Mexican and Texan traditions, with celebrations like Charro Days drawing the entire community together.

My trainer always liked to get his fuel bonus. So that meant when we were in Brownsville Texas or any place hot or cold he didn't run the engine for the air conditioner or the heater. So often we was always hot or cold depending on where we were.

This was a time before the APU was popular on tractors. APU's are common on road trucks with sleepers now. They have an auxiliary diesel engine that provides air conditioning and power to top off the batteries. They also provide electricity for a inverter, so the driver is able to run a microwave and a small refrigerator in his cab and other electronic devices.

Heat for the cab is often provided by a small diesel heater. These heaters are very fuel efficient and they use fuel from the tanks on the truck along with a small amount of electricity to operate the unit and circulate the warm air in the cab.

The very affordable Chinese versions of these heaters can be used virtually anywhere to heat small places. I have several that I use for rooms in my home.

When I was done training I got my own truck, and I did things a bit different. It was bad enough being away from the comforts of home and I didn't plan to freeze or to roast in a hot truck. Heck with the fuel bonus, I never got one.

 So I found myself in Kansas City Missouri in the winter at a railway station, waiting for my load to come in on the rail. I think I was there for at least two days, and I ran the truck to stay warm. So when I finally got my load and started on my way, sometime after that I had to fuel.
Now, when you fuel up a truck it normally asks you for your truck number, mileage, along with your trip number, and any other information your company may want. They see your mileage and the amount of fuel that you use, and calculate your miles per gallon. Also they can detect if someone is stealing fuel, if the numbers don't line up.

Well, my numbers didn't line up because of all the idling I had done while waiting for my load. The pump wouldn't let me pump any fuel until I worked it out with my company. I got on the phone with my company and said that I had idled my truck to stay warm while waiting for my load for those two days or so, and the person on the phone was not pleased to say the least.

He said, "you should get a bigger sleeping bag!" This didn't bother me at all, I could have cared less what he thought. This person on the other end of that phone goes home to a warm or cool house everyday, and I'm out here on this truck. I told him I'm not going to be uncomfortable in this truck and that I didn't care about the fuel bonus. I like to see that guy huddled up in a warm sleeping bag for 2 days and see how he likes it.

So before becoming a truck driver I was not a well traveled person. I really enjoyed going to these different places like Arizona, California, Midwest, Texas, and the deep south. I got to experience different food and went to all kinds of manufacturing plants. It was interesting.

There was a truck stop just off I-10 in Grosse Tete Louisiana that I found very interesting. It was a truck stop with a twenty four hour Cajun restaurant, gift shop, and it had a eighty foot by forty foot enclosure with live Siberian tigers. I remember getting the Cajun sampler in the restaurant and I enjoyed it. It was also very interesting to see the tigers, although the smell from their droppings was pretty bad.

Let's call this next story, " A Golden Opportunity."

One of the most peculiar and memorable moments of my trucking career happened during what should have been a routine pickup in Chicago. It was one of those days where everything felt more difficult than it needed to be. The pickup location was buried deep in the city, far from any convenient interstate. Navigating secondary roads with a tractor trailer is never easy, and Chicago's maze of tight streets and intersections didn't help. After a frustrating search, I finally found the plant, loaded up, and started the slow crawl back toward the highway.

At first, it seemed like just another day on the job. The usual grind of city driving, stopping at endless red lights, maneuvering through congested crossroads, and planning every turn with the precision of a surgeon. But about three or four miles from the plant, I noticed something unusual. A car was following me.

It didn't catch my attention right away. In a busy city, tailing vehicles are just part of the scenery. But this car was different. It wasn't just following, it was trying to get my attention. The driver flashed his headlights and blared his horn incessantly. At first I assumed it was just another impatient motorist upset that a slow moving truck was in their way. It happens all the time, drivers in cars don't understand the logistics of maneuvering a vehicle this size.

But this wasn't road rage. The car stuck close to my rear bumper, persistently flashing its lights and honking. I glanced in my mirrors and saw the driver frantically waving his arms, clearly trying to get me to pull over.

My mind raced. Did I hit something? Did something happen to my trailer? His behavior was frantic enough to suggest it was serious. But pulling over wasn't an option. Chicago's streets are not designed for the convenience of trucks, and there was no safe spot in sight.

The car stayed with me for miles. At every red light, it crept closer. At every stop, the driver leaned on his horn. Finally, I spotted a narrow shoulder and decided to pull over, even though it wasn't an ideal location. The man practically skidded to a stop behind me, jumping out of his car like his hair was on fire.

He approached my truck, red faced and breathless, his hands flailing like a man who'd just survived a catastrophe. When he started shouting, it wasn't about an accident or a safety issue. It was about the lawn.

"You ruined the lawn where you loaded up!" he bellowed. His voice was a mix of anger and desperation, and his words came tumbling out in an unfiltered tirade of curses.

For a moment I was stunned. I replayed the pickup in my mind, trying to remember if I had done anything out of the ordinary. The loading dock had been tight, and yes, I'd rolled onto the edge of the grass while backing in. But it hadn't struck me as a big deal at the time, just the kind of thing that happens in a cramped city loading zone.

The man wasn't just upset, he was demanding action. "Give me the number to your company!" he shouted. "You're gonna pay for this!"

I could see how worked up he was, but something about his intensity felt off. His rage didn't match the situation. I wasn't going to argue with him in the middle of the street, but I also wasn't going to hand over information without seeing the supposed damage for myself.

"I'll give you the number," I said, trying to stay calm, "but first, I'm going to turn around and go see what you're talking about."

He didn't seem happy with my answer, but I wasn't budging. After several more miles of navigating Chicago's chaotic streets, I found a spot where I could turn my truck around. It wasn't easy, city driving never is, but eventually, I made it back to the plant.

I parked, got out, and walked over to the lawn in question. There were faint tire tracks where I had backed in, but they were barely noticeable. The grass wasn't torn up, and there weren't any ruts. It was the kind of "damage" that would disappear with the next rain. Certainly not worth the kind of meltdown this man had thrown.

And then, as if the whole situation couldn't get stranger, I realized the man was gone.

I looked around for him, expecting him to be there waiting to prove his point. I even went inside the building to see if anyone knew who he was or what had happened, but it was like he'd vanished into thin air. No one seemed to know anything about him.

As I drove away, I couldn't shake the feeling that this had been about more than just tire tracks on a lawn. The man's desperation and fury made me wonder if he'd been trying to pull a scam. Maybe he thought he could intimidate me into giving him my company's information and use it to make a bogus claim. Maybe he was in some kind of financial trouble and saw an opportunity to exploit the situation.

I'll never know the full story. But the experience stayed with me, a reminder of the unpredictable nature of this job. Trucking isn't just about getting from point A to point B. It's about navigating the unexpected, dealing with people in all their complexity, and staying calm under pressure.

That day in Chicago taught me the importance of standing my ground and verifying the facts before reacting. It also left me wondering about the man who was so determined to make an issue out of nothing. What was his story? What was he trying to accomplish? I guess I'll never know. But every time I think about that day, I can't help but shake my head and laugh at the absurdity of it all.

Let's call this story, "The Dumb and the Detour, A Trucker's Guide to Yellowstone Misadventures"

Unfortunately, people do dumb things. Truck drivers are no exception, and I'm certainly not here to tell you that I was above it all. The truth is, I've done my fair share of questionable things in my time on the road. While youthful exuberance might explain some of it, age doesn't always guarantee wisdom either. But in this particular case, I was younger, cockier, and clearly not thinking things through. What I'm about to share with you is one of those stories, a particularly foolish decision I made that I certainly wouldn't recommend, nor would I ever attempt again.

Back then, I regularly hauled loads from Maine, out to Seattle Washington, and Pomona California. Once I dropped off the freight, I'd pick up another load and head back to Maine. It was a long grueling circuit, but I loved the freedom of the open road. Unlike many company drivers today, I didn't have electronic logs, GPS tracking, or rigidly pre-planned routes to worry about. My company trusted me to use my discretion, and while that might sound liberating, it also meant there was plenty of room for misjudgment.

On one particular trip, while heading back from Seattle to Maine, I got the brilliant idea to take a detour, one that would add significant and unnecessary miles to my trip. Why? Because I thought it would be nice to visit Yellowstone National Park. Now, don't get me wrong, Yellowstone is breathtaking. Its geysers, wildlife, and natural beauty are unlike anything else in the world. But deciding to veer that far off route in a fully loaded truck just to indulge my curiosity? That was as dumb as it sounds.

To make this happen, I had to plan carefully, or as carefully as one can when making a wildly irresponsible decision. I figured out how to get close enough to the park entrance while finding a place to drop my trailer. I can't for the life of me remember where I left it, but I know it wasn't exactly a sanctioned parking area. Once I unhooked, I bobtailed into the park, paid the entrance fees, and dove headfirst into playing tourist.

At first, it was everything I'd hoped for. The geysers, the bison, and the serene natural beauty, I was in awe. Yellowstone's vastness felt like an entirely different world compared to the monotony of the interstate. But here's the thing about awe, it has a funny way of making you forget about caution.

I vaguely recall the park rangers handing out pamphlets with all kinds of safety warnings. Don't approach wildlife. Don't get too close to the hot springs. Stay on marked paths. I must have skimmed it, tossed it aside, and thought, Yeah, yeah, I've got this. Spoiler alert, I didn't have this.

The first dumb thing I did? I walked up to a group of bison grazing peacefully. Let me tell you, bison are deceptively calm creatures. They're massive, majestic, and if you're an idiot like I was, you might think it's fine to get a little closer for a better look. So there I was, inching closer and closer, probably with the kind of confidence that only comes from ignorance, when one of them suddenly got up.

It didn't charge, it didn't stomp, it just looked at me. But that look said everything. It was a look that said, This far and no further, buddy. My heart leapt into my throat, and for a moment, I thought that was it for me.

Fortunately, I backed away, and the bison decided I wasn't worth the trouble. But let me tell you, that look stuck with me. I had to wonder how many other fools had gotten that same look before finding themselves on the wrong end of a bison's horns.

You'd think that experience would have knocked some sense into me, but no. I was on a roll. At one point, I wandered over to one of Yellowstone's famous hot springs. These things are gorgeous, brightly colored pools of boiling water surrounded by mineral deposits. The ground around them looks solid, but anyone who's read the safety warnings knows that it's often a thin crust, ready to give way at any moment.

Of course, I didn't let that stop me. I walked right up to the edge, completely oblivious to the danger. There I stood, staring into the steaming pool like an idiot, when it finally dawned on me, If this ground gives way, I'm dead. Falling into one of those springs isn't just a matter of getting wet, it's a matter of being boiled alive. The thought hit me like a ton of bricks, and I backed away as carefully as I could, heart pounding all the while.

When I think back on that trip to Yellowstone, I don't feel proud, I feel thankful to God. Thankful that the bison didn't charge, thankful that the ground didn't give way, and thankful that I didn't end up as a cautionary tale for future visitors.

Looking back I can't believe I jeopardized my own safety, and my job for a few hours of sightseeing. To make matters worse, I burned extra fuel, wasted time, and added miles to my route, all things that no responsible driver would do today. With the technology and oversight in modern trucking, I wouldn't have gotten away with it anyway.

But perhaps the biggest lesson I learned, is that being a commercial truck driver is more than just delivering loads or taking detours to satisfy your curiosity. It's about doing the right thing when nobody's watching, avoiding unnecessary risks, and maintaining professionalism.

So, if you're ever tempted to follow in my footsteps, let me save you the trouble, don't. Enjoy Yellowstone on your own time.

"Let's call this story, The Long Haul of Darkness, The Story of Bruce Mendenhall"

In the world of trucking, stories abound of long hours, isolated highways, and the camaraderie of fellow drivers. But every now and then, a darker tale emerges from the endless miles of asphalt, a story that reveals how the anonymity of life on the road can mask unimaginable horrors. Bruce Mendenhall's story is one of those tales, a chilling reminder of how even the most unassuming people can hide unspeakable secrets.

Bruce Mendenhall seemed like a typical truck driver. A man from Illinois, he spent decades behind the wheel, hauling freight across the United States. By all outward appearances, he was a quiet, hardworking individual, just another face among the countless truckers who keep the wheels of the nation's economy turning. But beneath his unremarkable exterior lay a man with a dark and violent obsession.

The string of crimes attributed to Mendenhall began to unravel in 2007, when the body of twenty five year old Sara Hulbert was discovered at a truck stop in Nashville Tennessee. Hulbert, a known sex worker, had been shot and left inside a truck stop parking lot. The case initially seemed like an isolated incident. Tragic, but not uncommon in the world of transient communities and vulnerable individuals. However, investigators soon began to connect her murder to a series of similar cases spanning multiple states.

The break in the case came when a truck stop surveillance camera captured Mendenhall's truck near the scene of Hulbert's murder. When police tracked him down and confronted him at another truck stop, they discovered blood evidence inside his cab, tying him not only to Hulbert but to several other unsolved cases. As authorities dug deeper, they uncovered a terrifying pattern of violence that suggested Mendenhall was a serial killer using his trucking career as a cover.

Mendenhall eventually confessed to killing multiple women, many of whom were sex workers or individuals living on the margins of society. His method was chillingly opportunistic. He would find his victims at truck stops, lure them into his truck, and murder them before disposing of their bodies along his routes. The transitory nature of his job made him difficult to track, as he rarely stayed in one place for long. Police suspect he may have been responsible for as many as nine murders, though the true number remains uncertain.

What makes Mendenhall's case particularly disturbing is how it highlights the vulnerabilities of life on the road. Truck stops, often isolated and poorly monitored, can become dangerous places for those who frequent them. The transient nature of trucking allows predators to move freely, exploiting the vastness of the country to commit crimes with little fear of immediate detection. Mendenhall's crimes exposed the dark underbelly of an industry that is otherwise vital to society.

Even after his arrest, Mendenhall continued to manipulate those around him. From his prison cell, he attempted to orchestrate a murder for hire plot targeting witnesses who could testify against him. This brazen act further demonstrated the cold and calculating nature of his character, showing that even confinement couldn't quell his dangerous impulses.

Bruce Mendenhall's story is a grim reminder that evil can lurk in the most unsuspecting places. For years, he drove the highways of America, delivering freight by day and committing heinous crimes under the cover of night. His case sent shockwaves through the trucking community, sparking conversations about safety, surveillance, and the unique vulnerabilities of life on the road.

While Mendenhall is now serving life in prison, the scars of his crimes remain. His story serves as both a cautionary tale and a call to action, a reminder of the need for vigilance and the importance of not taking the anonymity of the open road for granted. The highways may stretch endlessly into the horizon, but for some, they also hide the darkest corners of human nature.

The trucking industry, while vital to the economy, has always had its share of shadows. Beneath the surface of an industry that keeps the world moving lies a darker side, one where corruption, mob influence, and scandalous behavior have left their mark. It's a world that few openly talk about, but it's a part of trucking history and lore that adds an air of intrigue and caution to the profession. From organized crime syndicates infiltrating freight operations to high profile scandals involving embezzlement and exploitation, the trucking industry has seen its share of corruption and scandal.

One of the most infamous chapters in trucking history involves the influence of organized crime in freight operations during the mid 20th century. The Teamsters Union, one of the most powerful labor unions in American history, became deeply entwined with mob activity during its heyday. Under the leadership of Jimmy Hoffa, the Teamsters expanded rapidly, and with that expansion came allegations of corruption. Hoffa, a polarizing figure, was both revered for his dedication to workers' rights and reviled for his dealings with organized crime figures.

The mob's interest in the trucking industry was simple, control the movement of goods, and you control a significant portion of the economy. Mobsters used their influence within the Teamsters to secure sweetheart deals for businesses they controlled, extort money from trucking companies, and manipulate freight routes. Drivers and business owners who didn't comply often found themselves the victims of threats, sabotage, or worse. Trucks were burned, freight was hijacked, and in some cases, lives were lost.

One particularly scandalous story involves the murder of Anthony "Three Fingers" Castellito, a Teamsters official who opposed mob control of the union. Castellito's resistance to corruption led to his disappearance in 1961, and it was later revealed that he had been killed on orders from Anthony "Tony Pro" Provenzano, a mobster who held significant sway within the union. Castellito's death sent a chilling message to anyone who dared challenge the mob's grip on the trucking industry.

The connection between Hoffa and the mob remains one of the most enduring mysteries in American history. Hoffa's disappearance in 1975, widely believed to be the result of a mob hit, has never been solved. His legacy however, continues to cast a long shadow over the industry, serving as a cautionary tale about the dangers of power, corruption, and unchecked ambition.

Beyond mob influence, the trucking industry has also been the stage for major financial scandals. One of the most notable examples occurred in the 1990s, when executives at large trucking companies were caught inflating profits and falsifying financial records to deceive investors. The fraud, which involved major players in the logistics world, led to the collapse of several companies and significant financial losses for shareholders. Drivers and lower level employees often bore the brunt of these scandals, losing jobs and pensions while executives walked away with golden parachutes.

Corruption isn't limited to organized crime or corporate greed. Some of the darkest stories in trucking involve exploitation and human trafficking. Criminal networks have used the anonymity and mobility of the trucking industry to transport illegal goods and even people. Rest stops and truck stops, often isolated and poorly monitored, have been hotspots for illegal activity. While the majority of drivers are hardworking and honest, a small minority have been complicit in these crimes, either through active participation or by turning a blind eye.

One chilling example of exploitation involves the use of trucks to transport human trafficking victims. Criminal organizations have taken advantage of the vast network of highways and the transient nature of trucking to move people across state and international borders. These victims, often women and children, are subjected to unimaginable horrors, and the trucking industry has become an unintended facilitator of this dark trade. In recent years, organizations like Truckers Against Trafficking have worked to combat this issue, training drivers to recognize and report suspicious activity. Their efforts have saved lives and brought attention to a problem that thrives in the shadows.

Even local level corruption has plagued the trucking industry. In some cases, officials at weigh stations or regulatory agencies have been caught accepting bribes to overlook safety violations, allowing trucks with faulty brakes or overloaded trailers to continue on their way. These shortcuts can have deadly consequences, as poorly maintained or overloaded trucks are far more likely to cause accidents. For drivers who play by the rules, this kind of corruption creates an uneven playing field, rewarding those willing to cut corners at the expense of safety and integrity.

Then there are the more personal scandals, stories of drivers caught smuggling drugs, stealing freight, or engaging in elaborate schemes to defraud their employers. One infamous case involved a driver who stole an entire trailer of high end electronics and staged a fake hijacking to cover his tracks. The plot unraveled when investigators discovered inconsistencies in his story, leading to his arrest and the recovery of the stolen goods. While these stories are often sensationalized in the media, they represent a tiny fraction of the trucking workforce, most of whom are honest, hardworking individuals.

The dark side of trucking is a reminder that no industry is immune to corruption and crime. However, it also highlights the resilience and integrity of the vast majority of drivers and professionals who work tirelessly to keep goods moving across the country. For every story of scandal and corruption, there are countless untold stories of drivers who uphold the values of honesty, dedication, and hard work, even in the face of adversity.

As the trucking industry evolves, so too do the challenges it faces. Modern technology, from GPS tracking to electronic logging devices, has made it harder for bad actors to operate undetected. However, the industry must remain vigilant, addressing vulnerabilities and working to ensure that the dark shadows of the past do not obscure its bright future. Whether it's combating organized crime, cracking down on fraud, or rooting out exploitation, the fight for transparency and accountability in trucking is an ongoing journey. And like any good journey, it's one worth taking.

Modern Day Government Heavy Handedness, The Canadian Truckers' Convoy and Its Fallout.

Modern-day government heavy handedness was on full display during the Canadian trucker convoy of 2022, a massive protest that captured the world's attention and became a flashpoint in the ongoing debate about government overreach, individual freedoms, and civil disobedience. What began as a grassroots movement of truckers opposing vaccine mandates quickly evolved into a national and international conversation about the limits of state power, and the lengths to which governments might go to enforce compliance. The story of the convoy, and the government's response to it, remains a stark reminder of the tensions between authority and liberty in times of crisis.

The Freedom Convoy, as it came to be known, began as a protest against Canada's vaccine mandates for cross border truckers. In January 2022, the Canadian government introduced a policy requiring truck drivers crossing the U.S. Canada border to be fully vaccinated against COVID-19 or face quarantine upon returning to Canada. For an industry already reeling from driver shortages, long hours, and the pressures of supply chain disruptions, this mandate was seen by many as the last straw. The protest wasn't just about vaccines, it was about what many viewed as an overreach by a government that had spent two years implementing increasingly restrictive measures under the banner of public health.

Truckers from across the country began organizing, converging on Ottawa, the nation's capital, in late January. What started as a convoy of vehicles soon swelled into a massive demonstration, with thousands of truckers, their families, and supporters clogging the streets of downtown Ottawa. The convoy became a symbol of defiance against government mandates, attracting supporters from all walks of life, farmers, small business owners, and everyday Canadians fed up with restrictions they felt were infringing on their freedoms.

For weeks, the streets of Ottawa were filled with honking horns, waving flags, and impromptu speeches. The truckers set up camp, turning the city into a fortress of defiance. Protesters were largely peaceful, although their presence disrupted daily life in the city and drew criticism from those who felt the protests had gone too far. The movement gained international attention, with many outside Canada praising the truckers for standing up to what they viewed as authoritarian measures. However, it also faced condemnation from government officials, who described the protest as illegal and disruptive.

The government's response to the convoy marked a dramatic escalation in state intervention. Prime Minister Justin Trudeau invoked the Emergencies Act on February 14, 2022, the first time this law had been used in Canadian history. The Emergencies Act gave the government sweeping powers to freeze bank accounts, seize assets, and ban public gatherings associated with the protest. These measures were justified by the government as necessary to restore order, but they sparked outrage among civil liberties advocates and ordinary citizens alike.

One of the most controversial aspects of the government's response was the freezing of bank accounts belonging to protesters and their supporters. Under the Emergencies Act, financial institutions were ordered to identify and freeze accounts linked to individuals involved in the convoy. This included not only the truckers themselves but also anyone who had donated to the protest through crowdfunding platforms. The move was unprecedented, effectively cutting off individuals from their own money without due process. Many saw this as an alarming use of financial power to punish dissent and silence opposition.

For truckers already struggling with the financial hardships of their profession, losing access to their bank accounts was devastating. Some reported being unable to pay for fuel, food, or other necessities while stranded in Ottawa. Others feared long term consequences, such as being blacklisted by financial institutions or targeted for further government scrutiny. The freezing of accounts also had a chilling effect on public support for the protest, as many potential donors worried about facing similar repercussions.

The government's actions extended beyond financial measures. Protesters were forcibly removed from downtown Ottawa by police, who used pepper spray, tear gas, and batons to clear the streets. Trucks were towed, and many protesters were arrested, including high profile organizers of the convoy. The crackdown was widely broadcast, with images of police clashing with demonstrators sparking both condemnation and support, depending on one's perspective.

While the government's response was effective in ending the physical presence of the convoy in Ottawa, it also raised serious questions about the use of emergency powers in a democratic society. Critics argued that the invocation of the Emergencies Act was a gross overreach, setting a dangerous precedent for how governments could suppress dissent in the future. Civil liberties groups warned that targeting individuals' financial assets without judicial oversight represented a significant erosion of rights.

The convoy's legacy is complicated. For its supporters, it remains a symbol of resistance against government overreach and a rallying cry for freedom. The movement inspired similar protests in other countries, including the United States, where truckers organized convoys to protest mandates and restrictions. For its detractors, however, the convoy represented chaos, disruption, and a dangerous flirtation with extremism.

Regardless of where one stands on the issue, the Freedom Convoy and the government's response to it have left an indelible mark on Canadian society and the trucking industry. The events of 2022 highlighted the power of grassroots movements in an era of digital organization and crowdfunding, but they also revealed the lengths to which governments might go to maintain control. For truckers, the convoy was a reminder of their essential role in society, and the sacrifices they are often asked to make in the face of sweeping political decisions.

The Canadian truckers' convoy remains a polarizing moment in modern history, one that will be studied and debated for years to come. It serves as both a cautionary tale about the potential for government overreach and a testament to the power of ordinary people to stand up for what they believe in, even when the odds are stacked against them. Whether it ultimately changed anything or simply underscored existing divisions, it's clear that the echoes of this protest will resonate long after the last truck has left the streets of Ottawa.

A Brighter Side of Commercial Driving, Stories of Kindness, Community, and Ministry on the Road.

Now, let's look at a brighter side of commercial driving. While it's easy to focus on the challenges, corruption, or hardships within the industry, the truth is that the road is also filled with countless acts of kindness, camaraderie, and even ministry. Commercial drivers aren't just moving freight or passengers, they're often the unsung heroes of the highways, using their unique position to make a difference in the lives of others. From drivers offering a helping hand to their fellow travelers to those turning their time on the road into a ministry of hope, the stories of goodness in the driving industry shine just as brightly as the headlights piercing through the night.

One shining example of kindness in the industry is the phenomenon of truckers helping stranded motorists. Imagine being stuck on the side of the road late at night, your car broken down and the nearest help miles away. For many stranded drivers, the sight of a semi pulling over is a beacon of hope. Commercial drivers, with their extensive knowledge of the road and mechanical know how, often stop to assist in ways that go far beyond what's expected. Whether it's changing a flat tire, providing a phone for an emergency call, or simply staying until help arrives, these drivers embody the spirit of the road. One particularly heartwarming story involves a driver who stopped to help a young family whose car had overheated on a desert highway. Not only did he help them fix the issue, but he also gave the kids snacks and cold water from his truck, turning a potentially frightening experience into one of gratitude and relief.

The driving industry has also become a platform for ministry and acts of faith. Many drivers use their time on the road to serve as a source of encouragement and hope for others. Ministries like Transport for Christ and Truckers Chapel cater specifically to the trucking community, offering spiritual guidance and a place for drivers to find solace in their hectic schedules. These mobile chapels, often housed in converted trailers at truck stops, provide services, prayer, and even counseling for drivers who need a moment of peace or a listening ear. Drivers themselves often take on the role of ministers in their own way, offering words of encouragement to fellow truckers over CB radios or sharing their faith during coffee breaks at rest stops. For many, the isolation of the road becomes an opportunity to reflect, connect, and uplift others in ways they might not have imagined when they first started driving.

One remarkable story of ministry on the road involves a truck driver named Ron, who turned his rig into a rolling food pantry. During his hauls across the Midwest, Ron began noticing just how many small communities were struggling with food insecurity. Instead of simply driving by, he decided to take action. With the support of his local church and a network of fellow drivers, he started filling his trailer with donated food items, delivering them to food banks and shelters in towns along his route. Over time, his efforts grew into a full blown operation, with other drivers volunteering to transport goods and businesses pitching in with supplies. Ron's story is a testament to how the trucking community can mobilize to make a real impact, using their unique access to the country's highways to bring hope and sustenance to those in need.

Goodness in the driving industry isn't limited to grand gestures, it often comes in the form of small, everyday acts of humanity. Drivers frequently share their resources with one another, whether it's lending a tool for a quick repair, buying a meal for someone who's short on cash, or simply offering a friendly conversation to break up the monotony of the road. One heartwarming tradition is the "trucker wave," a simple hand gesture exchanged between drivers passing each other. It's a small but powerful reminder that, even in the vastness of the open road, no one is truly alone.

The industry also has its share of uplifting stories involving bus drivers. One well known example is the story of a school bus driver who noticed a child on her route was coming to school without adequate winter clothing. Instead of ignoring the situation, she quietly bought the child a new coat, gloves, and a hat, ensuring they would be warm during the cold months. When asked about it later, she simply said, "It was the right thing to do." Stories like this highlight the compassion and attentiveness that many drivers bring to their work, showing that their responsibilities go far beyond simply getting from point A to point B.

Community support is another bright spot in the driving world. Truckers frequently band together in times of crisis, using their resources and networks to help others. After natural disasters like hurricanes or wildfires, truck drivers are often the first to step up, volunteering to deliver essential supplies to affected areas. Their ability to navigate difficult terrain and organize on short notice makes them invaluable during emergencies. In one notable instance, a convoy of truckers delivered clean drinking water to a town where the municipal supply had been contaminated, earning them heartfelt thanks from the residents.

Even in more personal, one on one situations, drivers are known for going above and beyond. One story that gained attention involved a driver who helped a fellow trucker suffering from a medical emergency at a rest stop. The driver not only called for help but stayed by his side, talking to him and keeping him calm until paramedics arrived. These moments of kindness, though they may seem small, have a profound impact on the people involved, fostering a sense of connection and humanity in an industry often characterized by long hours of solitude.

These stories remind us that the driving industry is about so much more than logistics and schedules. It's about people, people who care for one another, who take time out of their busy lives to make a difference, and who understand the value of kindness and community. Whether it's through ministry, volunteer efforts, or simple acts of compassion, the brighter side of commercial driving is a testament to the good that can be found on the road. It's a world where even the hum of an engine can carry the sound of hope, and every mile traveled brings the opportunity to make someone's day a little better.

I will call this next story "An Uninvited Guest". I was in my truck, stopped at toll booth for the Mackinac bridge on the southern side, on a cold winter day. The bridge spans the distance between the cities of St. Ignace and Mackinaw City in Michigan and the upper and lower peninsulas of the state. The Mackinac bridge is the longest suspension bridge in the western hemisphere. The total length of the Mackinac bridge is 26,372 ft.

After I paid my toll some guy jumped out of nowhere onto my driver side step and hung on to my mirror bracket. He wanted something, maybe it was money for drugs or something, I can't remember what.

I was startled, and with my window still up, I yelled at the man to get off. I wasn't about to open the window or the door because I didn't know what his intentions were.

I quickly decided that if he wasn't going to get off my truck then he was gonna go for a very cold ride over the bridge. I took off as fast as I could, hitting the air horn and grabbing gears. Perhaps the site of a man hanging off a truck and the sound of the loud air horn would get somebody's attention.

The look on the man's face morphed from determined to downright horrified. The cold wind whipped around him, making his eyes water as if he was watching the end of a sad movie. By midway point of the bridge, the guy looked like he'd been flash frozen for freshness. His earlier enthusiasm was gone, replaced by chattering of teeth, and he held on so tight I thought he'd fuse with the truck. It must have dawned on him that this wasn't so smart after all. I finally reached the other side of the bridge where I stopped and he got off, and shuffled away without a problem.

Time to shift rides now and hear some stories from my time as a tour bus driver, I'll call this one "The Fuhrer", the German word meaning leader or guide, the title Adolf Hitler adopted for himself.

My bus assignment was a multi day Fall foliage sightseeing trip with people from Germany. I arrived at Logan airport early in the afternoon where my German speaking tour guide got on the bus. She was a small older German woman who lived here in the United States.

Soon the plane arrived with the people from Germany ready to take their tour.

Although I never said it to the woman, in my mind I thought of her as the Fuhrer. She wasn't much of a people person. I found her kind of hard to get along with. She kind of bossed everybody around and made the people keep their same seats each day in the bus for the duration of the trip.

At the end of the trip she had what seemed to be a prepared speech to the people about how important the tip was for her and myself. I don't really like that myself. I'm old school I guess. I remember when the tip was given because you especially liked whatever service you got and it wasn't mandatory. Really, why call it a tip if it's mandatory. Just include it in the bill then. So I didn't really like that when tour guides ask for tips. Anyway, we did end up getting a rather large tip at the end.

The most notable thing the Fuhrer did on the trip was when she used a permanent marker to Mark numbers above each row of seats. I guess she couldn't find the numbers that were already there. Rather than asking me about if she could number the seats she just went ahead and did it.

When I told the owner of the bus company what she did, he wasn't happy. She had to pay quite a bit to get that removed.

The next story I will call " A Crappy Ride". While driving a bus load of people to The Hilltop Steakhouse in Saugus Massachusetts we found ourselves in a big traffic backup on Rt. 1. This was not at all unusual but what followed was.

 At first, it was just a whisper of a whiff, a gentle nudge at the nostrils. But then, oh boy, it escalated into a full blown nasal assault! I'm thinking, oh no!, someone crapped themselves!

Perhaps I had an immature moment but I couldn't help thinking it was hilarious. Meanwhile, I could tell the rest of the passengers were getting restless. You could see the irritation brewing like a storm cloud.

Trying to keep my straight face was futile. I quickly slid open my side window for some fresh air and burst out laughing. Yeah, not really funny though, I guess the man who crapped himself had some physical or mental deficiencies.

It was his friend that sat beside him that got him to go on this trip to get him out of the house. Now he was helping his friend clean up best they could in the tiny bathroom in the back of the bus with no water to wash. Not fun. But hey, "stuff" happens . .

 Will call the next story "Hoops And Hiccups".

 I accepted the assignment. I was on my way to a Boston college to pick up a basketball team and its coach. From there we would go to upstate New York where the team would play a game and we'd spend the night there and then come back the next day, at least that was the plan.

The game they played was an utter failure, they lost bad. The coach was mad, and with a raised voice he used choice words on his teammates.

After the game we drove an hour or two to the motel that we were going to stay at, and then I took the group to a bar where they stayed till closing, then it was back to the motel.

 Later the next morning the coach could be heard with a raised voice cussing out one or more of the teammates in the lobby of the motel. Meanwhile, across the lobby seated with a cup of tea and a barely touched croissant, sat an older woman. Her morning repose was obviously rudely interrupted by every expletive that was echoed. She got up and abruptly marched toward coach.

She said, "excuse me, young man . . Do you kiss your mother with that same mouth?", stepping forward with a stern look that could wilt flowers. The coach turning abruptly with a confusing look on his face, mumbled something unintelligible. The older woman continued, "if I had a dollar for every swear word you just said, I could retire comfortably".

 The coach blinked, the team tried their hardest to stifle their laughs, their attention now fully shifted from their coaches tirade to this unexpected showdown. At this point, the coach's face matched the hue of the hotel's lavish red curtains. The team, seizing their chance, scattered towards the breakfast buffet like pigeons at the site of breadcrumbs. And just like that, piece was restored.

 The rest of that day for me consisted of driving the team around to run errands, like washing their clothes at a laundromat, and some shopping and whatnot. They had me running around all day and then come evening they wanted me to drive them back to Boston while they slept on the bus.

 Apparently the coach didn't care anything about me the driver, or about my sleep. Also he was completely ignorant about hours of service regulations that I had to comply with, and a pesky thing called a log book.

Obviously it's not in my best interest to argue with customers, but now it was my turn to tell him off. I told him in no uncertain terms that we was not going and that we would sleep here and leave in the morning and that's what we did.

This last story that I want to include in this book about my time driving tour bus is certainly not funny. Let's call it, "Detours Of Memory."

The assignment consisted of five tour buses shuttling school sports teams and their coaches and some parents from a motel in upstate New York to a sports arena about 5 miles away. This went on for a few days, back and forth from the motel to the sports arena and occasionally out to a restaurant.

We was getting near to the end of our assignment when one group of people that were on a particular bus didn't want to ride on that bus anymore.

I remember being in the lobby and phone calls were being made and people were milling around murmuring. I didn't know what was going on. The only information that I knew is that this particular group of people didn't want to ride on the bus that was assigned to them anymore, and that's all I knew.

Pulling one of the coaches aside, I told her that I had to know what was going on because my superiors would want to know the issue from the perspective of the other drivers as well as the passengers.

She explained that their bus driver would often get lost even though he was going to the same place each time and they felt their safety could be in jeopardy.

I felt bad for the bus driver. He was an older gentleman and was probably experiencing an age related cognitive issue. I don't know what happened beyond that, but that certainly could be the end of his career.

The Bizarre Side of the Road. Strange Tales from the World of Commercial Driving.

I don't think this book would be complete without looking into the bizarre. Maybe it's the countless hours I've spent alone on the road, or perhaps I've listened to a little too much Art Bell and his late night discussions of the weird and unexplained. But let's face it, the trucking industry has its fair share of strange stories. From UFO encounters and unexplained lights to peculiar cargo and eerie coincidences, the open road has a way of giving you stories that make you question reality. Whether these tales are true or just tall trucker tales, I'll leave that up to you to decide. But buckle up, because this ride gets weird.

One of the most infamous stories involves a trucker in Nevada who swears he encountered a UFO while hauling a load late at night through the desolate highways near Area 51. According to his account, the cab's radio started picking up static, and his CB, which had been silent for hours, suddenly crackled with an unfamiliar voice repeating coordinates in a robotic tone. At first, he assumed it was a glitch or prank, but as he approached the location, he noticed bright unnatural lights on the horizon. Thinking it might be a helicopter or some military operation, he kept driving, only to have the lights suddenly hover directly above his rig. The light was so intense that it illuminated the entire cab, making it seem like daylight for a brief moment.

Then, just as suddenly, the lights vanished, and his truck shut down completely, engine, lights, everything. After what felt like an eternity, his truck roared back to life, and he floored it until he reached the next truck stop. There, he found two other drivers talking about seeing strange lights in the same area. While skeptics chalk it up to overactive imaginations or the military testing something experimental, the driver insists he felt something "off," as if he was being watched. To this day, he avoids that stretch of highway whenever possible.

Not all bizarre tales involve UFOs or the unexplained. Sometimes, the strange comes from the cargo itself. One legendary story is about a trucker who was hired to transport a sealed trailer from a remote lab in the Midwest to an undisclosed location on the East Coast. The job came with strict instructions: do not stop, do not open the trailer, and do not ask questions. Naturally, curiosity got the better of him during a quick stop to refuel. As he leaned close to the trailer, he heard a faint scratching sound, like something alive inside. Startled, he asked the dispatch for more information, only to be told to keep moving and not to worry about it.

Later that night, while driving through a foggy stretch of road, the scratching grew louder, and the entire trailer began to shake. Convinced that whatever was inside might pose a danger, he pulled over and decided to take a look. Opening the trailer just a crack, he was greeted with a pair of glowing eyes staring back at him. Panicked, he slammed the door shut and drove straight to the delivery point without another pause. To this day, he claims not to know what he was hauling, but the experience left him so rattled that he never took another "no questions asked" job again. Another bizarre story involves a trucker driving through the Deep South late one night when he came across an elderly hitchhiker on a deserted stretch of road. Against his better judgment, he decided to give the man a ride. The hitchhiker, dressed in outdated clothing and carrying an old suitcase, didn't say much at first, but as the drive went on, he began recounting chillingly accurate details about the trucker's life, things he couldn't possibly know. The driver, increasingly unnerved, asked the man who he was, but the hitchhiker simply smiled and said, "You'll know soon enough."

When the driver glanced at his passenger again, the seat was empty. Startled, he stopped the truck, convinced the man must have fallen out or jumped, but there was no sign of him anywhere on the road. The suitcase however, remained in the cab. Despite his fear, the trucker opened it, only to find it empty. He later discovered that the stretch of road where he'd picked up the hitchhiker was notorious for ghostly sightings, with similar stories of phantom passengers dating back decades.

Finally, there's the story of a refrigerated trucker who was tasked with delivering a load to a remote facility in the middle of the desert. When he arrived, the facility appeared abandoned, with rusted gates and overgrown weeds. But as he waited, a group of men in dark suits emerged from a nondescript building, carrying what looked like biohazard equipment. Without a word, they directed him to unload the trailer into a massive cold storage unit. The entire operation was done in silence, and the trucker was paid in cash, far more than the job was worth. Years later, he read a news report about mysterious biological experiments allegedly conducted at that location. He has wondered ever since, if he unknowingly delivered something far more dangerous than frozen goods.

The open road has a way of amplifying the strange. Maybe it's the isolation, the endless hours to think, or just the kinds of characters you meet along the way. Whatever the case, these stories remind us that trucking isn't just a job, it's an adventure, one with twists, turns, and occasional glimpses into the bizarre. Whether you believe them or not, these tales add a little extra flavor to the rich tapestry of life on the road. So the next time you hear a strange noise in your cab or see a flicker of light on the horizon, remember, out here, anything is possible.

There are many books that you can read about the world of commercial driving, offering insights into the lives of truck and bus drivers, the challenges they face, and the stories they create on the road. These books range from personal memoirs to industry guides, each shedding light on an often misunderstood profession. Whether you're looking for practical advice or simply a good story, the literature surrounding commercial driving offers something for everyone.

One of the classics in this genre is "Big Rig. Trucking and the Decline of the American Dream" by Steve Viscelli. This book explores the economic and social forces that shape the trucking industry, delving into how deregulation and corporate practices have impacted drivers' lives. Viscelli, a sociologist, takes an academic yet accessible approach, blending research with interviews from real drivers. The book paints a vivid picture of the struggles many truckers face, from long hours to low pay, and challenges readers to consider the human cost of the goods they consume.

For those who prefer a more personal perspective, "Semi-True Tales of a Regular Guy" by Jeff Clark is a must read. Clark, a veteran truck driver, recounts his experiences on the road with humor, candor, and a touch of nostalgia. The book is filled with colorful anecdotes about life behind the wheel, offering a glimpse into the camaraderie and solitude that come with the job. Clark's stories are as entertaining as they are enlightening, making this book a favorite among both drivers and general readers.

Another compelling read is "Trucking Country: The Road to America's Wal-Mart Economy" by Shane Hamilton. This book delves into the history of trucking, tracing its evolution from a small scale, independent operation to a highly regulated and corporatized industry. Hamilton connects the rise of trucking to broader economic trends, including the dominance of big box retailers like Wal-Mart. The book is a fascinating exploration of how the trucking industry has shaped, and been shaped by, the American economy.

For those interested in the world of buses, "The Bus Driver Who Wanted to Be God" by Etgar Keret offers a quirky and thought provoking collection of short stories, one of which revolves around a bus driver who takes his job very seriously. While not a traditional book about commercial driving, Keret's imaginative storytelling offers a unique lens through which to view the responsibilities and quirks of life as a driver.

For aspiring truck drivers or those looking to improve their skills, "CDL Study Guide 2024, Commercial Driver's License Training Guide" is an invaluable resource. This comprehensive guide covers everything from basic road safety to advanced driving techniques, helping readers prepare for their CDL exams. While it's not a narrative book, its practical advice and clear explanations make it an essential tool for anyone entering the field.

Finally, "One for the Road: Hitchhiking Through the Australian Outback" by Tony Horwitz offers an outsider's perspective on life on the road, including interactions with truck drivers. While not exclusively about commercial driving, Horwitz's journey through remote stretches of Australia highlights the unique challenges faced by truckers in isolated regions. His encounters with drivers reveal the humor, grit, and resilience that define the profession, even in the most rugged conditions.

These books, each in their own way, illuminate the complexities and rewards of commercial driving. They capture the grit, resilience, and humanity of the men and women who keep the wheels of the world turning, offering readers a deeper appreciation for the industry and its people. Whether you're a driver yourself or simply curious about life on the road, these stories and guides provide a window into an endlessly fascinating world.

There are many movies that you can watch that delve into the world of commercial driving, capturing the grit, danger, and camaraderie that come with life on the road. From heart pounding thrillers to heartfelt dramas, these films showcase the unique challenges and stories that emerge from driving trucks or buses. They offer glimpses into the lives of those behind the wheel, blending action, humor, and human emotion into compelling narratives.

One of the most iconic films in this category is Steven Spielberg's "Duel." This 1971 thriller tells the story of a businessman driving through the California desert who becomes the target of a relentless, faceless truck driver. The enormous, rusting semi becomes a character in its own right, embodying menace and mystery. With almost no dialogue from the antagonist, the film creates a sense of suspense that keeps viewers on edge. "Duel" captures the isolation and unpredictability of the road, making it a must watch for anyone intrigued by trucking's darker side.

Another unforgettable entry is "Convoy," a 1978 action film directed by Sam Peckinpah. Based on the hit country song by C.W. McCall, the movie follows a group of truckers led by "Rubber Duck," played by Kris Kristofferson. The convoy starts as a form of solidarity against a corrupt sheriff but soon grows into a larger movement, capturing the rebellious spirit of the trucking community. The film's mix of humor, action, and social commentary makes it a cult classic that celebrates the camaraderie and defiance of truck drivers.

For a more dramatic take, "Sorcerer" 1977, directed by William Friedkin, explores the harrowing world of transporting hazardous materials. The story follows four men from different parts of the world, each with a dark past, as they are hired to drive unstable explosives through treacherous South American terrain. The film's tension is palpable, with scenes that highlight the immense skill and nerve required to handle such dangerous cargo. "Sorcerer" is a masterclass in suspense and an homage to the resilience of those who take on high stakes driving jobs.

If you're looking for a lighter tone, "Smokey and the Bandit" 1977, is a classic comedy that captures the fun and chaos of the open road. Burt Reynolds stars as "The Bandit," a charismatic trucker hired to transport a shipment of beer across state lines, all while evading the relentless Sheriff Buford T. Justice. With its fast paced chases, witty banter, and sense of adventure, the film became a cultural phenomenon and remains a beloved depiction of trucking hijinks.

On the bus driving side, "Speed" 1994, starring Keanu Reeves and Sandra Bullock, is an adrenaline fueled thriller that centers around a city bus rigged with a bomb. The premise is simple yet gripping, if the bus slows below fifty miles per hour, the bomb will detonate. As the driver,

Bullock's character becomes an unlikely hero, navigating through chaos to keep passengers alive. The film highlights the intense responsibility bus drivers carry while delivering edge of your seat action.

A lesser known gem is "The Wages of Fear" 1953, a French Italian classic that served as the inspiration for "Sorcerer." It tells the story of four desperate men hired to transport two trucks of nitroglycerin across rugged terrain. With every bump in the road threatening catastrophe, the film is a nerve wracking exploration of courage, greed, and human endurance. Its stark portrayal of the risks faced by drivers hauling hazardous materials resonates even decades later.

For a more contemporary perspective, "Hell Drivers" 1957, a British film, dives into the competitive and dangerous world of gravel haulers. The story follows Tom Yately, a new recruit in a cutthroat trucking company where drivers push themselves to dangerous extremes to meet quotas. The film explores themes of exploitation, loyalty, and redemption, offering a gritty look at the darker side of the trucking industry.

Finally, for a dose of humor and heart, "The Bus Driver" 2016, is an independent film from Taiwan that blends comedy and social commentary. It tells the story of a small town bus driver who becomes entangled in a community scandal. While not as well known as other films in this genre, it offers a unique cultural perspective on the role of a driver and their impact on the people they serve.

These films, spanning decades and genres, bring the world of commercial driving to life. They explore the challenges, triumphs, and dangers faced by those who navigate the open road, offering something for everyone, from high speed thrills to quiet moments of reflection. Whether you're a driver yourself or simply a fan of stories about the road, these movies capture the essence of life behind the wheel.

Songs of the Open Road: A Tribute to Trucking and Commercial Driving
This book would not be complete without a deep dive into the songs that

celebrate, romanticize, and sometimes lament the life of commercial driving. Few professions have inspired as much music as trucking, and for good reason. The long hours, endless highways, and solitary nature of the job create a perfect backdrop for storytelling. Country music, in particular, has embraced the trucking lifestyle, producing some of the most iconic anthems that resonate with drivers and fans alike. These songs capture the essence of the open road, the camaraderie of truck stops, the yearning for home, and the pride of keeping the world moving. Let's explore some of the most memorable songs written about commercial driving, along with the stories behind them.

Perhaps the most iconic trucking song is "Convoy" by C.W. McCall, written by McCall and Chip Davis in 1975. This song became an instant classic, capturing the spirit of the CB radio craze and the rebellious streak of independent truckers. The song tells the story of a group of truckers forming a massive convoy to defy speed limits, weigh stations, and the law itself. With its catchy chorus and vivid storytelling, "Convoy" not only became a No. 1 hit on both the country and pop charts but also sparked a cultural phenomenon, including a movie adaptation. It remains a staple for anyone who's ever dreamed of freedom on the highway.

Another timeless anthem is "Six Days on the Road" by Dave Dudley, released in 1963. Written by Earl Green and Carl Montgomery, this song is often regarded as the first true trucking song, setting the stage for the genre. The lyrics tell the story of a weary trucker heading home after six long days on the road, dodging weigh stations and dreaming of his return. Dudley's gravelly voice and the song's driving rhythm perfectly capture the grit and determination of a trucker's life, making it a favorite among drivers to this day.

Red Sovine's "Teddy Bear" is a heart wrenching ballad that brings a softer, more emotional touch to the trucking genre. Released in 1976, the song tells the story of a young boy, nicknamed Teddy Bear, who communicates with truckers over a CB radio after losing his father, a truck driver, in an accident. The truckers rally together to bring joy to

Teddy Bear, creating a powerful narrative about the kindness and camaraderie of the trucking community. Sovine's storytelling and the song's emotional depth have made it a classic that continues to resonate.

Merle Haggard's "Movin' On" is another standout, written as the theme song for the 1974 TV show of the same name about two truckers navigating life on the road. Haggard's lyrics celebrate the resilience and independence of truckers, capturing the pride and determination that define the profession. The upbeat tempo and Haggard's unmistakable voice make this song a celebration of the open road and the people who keep the wheels turning.

Kathy Mattea's "Eighteen Wheels and a Dozen Roses" brings a touch of romance and nostalgia to the trucking world. Written by Paul Nelson and Gene Nelson, the song tells the story of a trucker on his last run before retiring, dreaming of spending his golden years with his wife. Released in 1988, the song became a No. 1 country hit, capturing the beauty of life's transitions and the sacrifices made by those who dedicate their lives to the road.

Johnny Cash, a master storyteller, contributed to the genre with "Big Wheels Rollin'." While not as widely known as some of his other hits, this song showcases Cash's knack for capturing the rugged beauty of blue collar life. The lyrics reflect the perseverance and pride of truck drivers, highlighting their essential role in keeping the economy moving.

The humor and grit of trucker culture are captured in Jerry Reed's "East Bound and Down," the theme song for the 1977 film Smokey and the Bandit. Written by Reed and Dick Feller, the song is an adrenaline fueled anthem about hauling beer across state lines while evading law enforcement. Reed's lively performance, and the song's high energy tempo perfectly complement the movie's fast paced action, making it a beloved trucking anthem.

For those who enjoy a touch of outlaw spirit, "Truck Drivin' Man" by Terry Fell is a classic honky tonk ode to life behind the wheel. Released in

1954, it's one of the earliest examples of a trucking song, with lyrics that celebrate the joys and struggles of the open road. The song has been covered by numerous artists, including Buck Owens and Willie Nelson, cementing its place in trucking music history.

"Phantom 309" by Red Sovine offers a ghostly twist on the trucking genre. This haunting tale recounts a trucker's encounter with a mysterious driver named Big Joe, who gives him a ride on a stormy night. The next day, the narrator learns that Big Joe died years earlier in a heroic accident. The story's eerie charm and Sovine's heartfelt delivery make it a favorite among fans of trucking lore.

Modern artists have also embraced the trucking genre. Brad Paisley's "Mud on the Tires" might not focus solely on commercial driving, but its celebration of hitting the road and exploring new places resonates with anyone who loves life behind the wheel. Similarly, Alabama's "Roll On Eighteen Wheeler" tells the story of a trucker's family waiting anxiously for his safe return, blending themes of family, resilience, and the dangers of the job.

These songs, and countless others, form the soundtrack of the trucking industry. They capture the spirit of the open road, the camaraderie of the profession, and the sacrifices made by those who spend their lives behind the wheel. Whether you're a driver yourself or just a fan of good storytelling, these songs remind us of the humanity and adventure that define the world of commercial driving. They're a tribute to the men and women who keep the world moving, one mile and one melody at a time.

5 OWNER OPERATORS

Thinking about owning your own truck? This is certainly possible. This can be a rewarding venture that offers greater Independence and the potential for increased earnings. However, the process of transitioning from a truck driver to an owner operator requires careful planning and consideration.

This chapter will guide you through the steps involved in buying a truck and becoming an owner operator. Obviously you'll want to do your research carefully on the type of trucking you want to do, and the cost associated with owning and operating your own truck. Consider factors such as the type of truck you need, and all the necessary permits and requirements. Determine how much you're willing to invest in buying a truck and starting your own business as an owner operator. Consider expenses such as the cost of the truck, insurance, maintenance, fuel, permits, taxes, and other operating costs. Keep in mind that companies with multiple trucks get discounts on registration, insurance, etc. It's crucial to have a clear understanding of your financial capabilities and limitations.

If you don't have enough capital to purchase a truck outright, you may need to explore financing options such as loans or leasing. Compare interest rates, terms, and conditions from different lenders to find the most suitable financing option for your situation. Ensure that you can comfortably manage the monthly payments without straining your finances. Obtain necessary permits such as a motor carrier authority MC number, unified carrier registration UCR, international registration plan IRP, and international fuel tax agreement IFTA. Ensure that you will comply with all regulatory requirements to avoid fines or penalties.

As an owner operator, your success will depend on your dedication, professionalism, and work ethic. Uphold high standards of service, prioritize safety, and build a reputation for reliability and efficiency. By delivering exceptional service, you can build long term relationships with clients and secure repeat business.

Fortunately, there are a variety of training resources available to help aspiring owner operators make the transition successfully. From specialized schools to books and online courses, these resources provide the knowledge and tools you need to navigate the challenges of running your own trucking business.

One of the most comprehensive ways to prepare for the owner operator lifestyle is through specialized training programs offered by trucking schools and organizations. While most CDL schools focus on basic driver training, some programs go a step further, offering courses tailored specifically for those looking to become independent operators. These courses often cover topics like truck maintenance, cost management, contract negotiation, and compliance with Department of Transportation DOT regulations. Schools such as the National Tractor Trailer School NTTS, and Roadmaster Drivers School provide not only CDL training but also workshops on business fundamentals for those interested in going independent. Some community colleges and technical schools also offer business courses designed for small business owners, which can be invaluable for understanding book keeping, taxes, and legal compliance.

For those who prefer self guided learning, books can be an excellent resource. One of the most highly recommended titles is "The Successful Truck Owner Operator" by Ken R. Laws. This book is packed with practical advice on everything from choosing the right truck to managing expenses and understanding freight lanes. Laws draws on decades of experience to offer insights that are both actionable and realistic. Another must read is "Make More Money with Your Trucking Business" by Jimmy Cox. This book takes a deep dive into the financial side of trucking, emphasizing how to maximize profits while minimizing risks.

For a broader understanding of the industry, "How to Become an Independent Owner Operator Truck Driver" by Jeffrey A. Meyer offers a step by step guide to starting and running your own operation, making it a great resource for beginners.

In addition to books, many online platforms offer training specifically for aspiring owner operators. Websites like Trucker Path and TruckingTruth have entire sections dedicated to resources for independent drivers, including forums where experienced owner operators share advice and answer questions. Online courses like those offered by Trucking Business Academy provide structured lessons on topics like dispatching, finding loads, and understanding freight brokerage. These courses often include video tutorials, downloadable materials, and even one-on-one coaching sessions, making them an excellent option for those who prefer interactive learning.

Another valuable resource is the Owner Operator Independent Drivers Association OOIDA, a nonprofit organization dedicated to representing the interests of independent truckers. OOIDA offers a wealth of training materials, including webinars, workshops, and written guides. Their business services team can help new owner operators with everything from insurance selection to tax preparation, ensuring you're set up for success from day one.

Practical training isn't limited to formal courses or books. Many seasoned owner operators recommend spending time working closely with an experienced mentor. Some trucking companies encourage this by offering mentorship programs where you can learn the ropes of managing your own truck while still working as a company driver. Observing how an experienced owner operator handles maintenance schedules, navigates freight markets, and maintains profitability can provide insights you simply can't get from books or courses.

Beyond learning the operational and financial aspects of running a trucking business, understanding the technology side is increasingly important. Modern trucking relies heavily on apps and software for everything from finding loads to tracking expenses. Apps like DAT Load Board, Truckstop.com, and KeepTruckin' are essential tools for owner operators. Learning how to use these platforms effectively can make a huge difference in your bottom line, so taking the time to explore tutorials and guides on these technologies is highly recommended.

Finally, don't underestimate the power of networking. Attending trucking expos, trade shows, and industry events can connect you with experienced professionals who can offer valuable advice and guidance. Events like the Mid America Trucking Show MATS often feature seminars and workshops tailored to owner operators, covering topics like fuel efficiency, legal updates, and the latest in trucking technology. These events are also great opportunities to meet potential partners, suppliers, or even find deals on equipment.

Becoming an owner operator is a challenging but rewarding endeavor. It's not just about driving, it's about running a business, managing risks, and constantly adapting to changes in the industry. With the right training resources, you can build a strong foundation that sets you up for long term success. Whether you choose to attend a specialized school, dive into books and online courses, or seek mentorship from experienced drivers, the knowledge you gain will be invaluable as you embark on this new chapter of your trucking career.

6 SAFETY FIRST

"Safety is more important than convenience", Don Hambidge. Safety should be on our mind no matter what type of vehicle we drive.

I have seen for myself lots of accidents in my time as a commercial driver, and heard stories of many more.

Let's differentiate between low speed accidents with minor property damage from backing, and fender benders, to high speed accidents that often cause injury and death. Big difference here, I have had many backing accidents where there was minor property damage, but I've been very fortunate, and I thank God that I haven't been involved in any serious high speed accident.

You got to keep in mind that no matter how safe you're driving is, the possibility of a high speed accident with injury or death is always possible. Of course by safe driving you can minimize accidents, but you can't control other people, and phenomena that can occur.

Also, while backing accidents that cause minor property damage are more common, and I don't know any drivers who never had one, too many of these in a short amount of time will put you out of a job. So exercise common sense when you're performing your backing maneuvers. Get out and look when you need to. If you have barn doors on your trailer make sure they stay open as you bump the dock. Door hold back systems seem to fail at the most inappropriate time, and I have taken off my fair share of doors through the years.

I'll devote the rest of this chapter to the more important topic of high speed accidents that produce more property damage, injury, and death. You don't have to look very hard to see people driving unsafely. Just go out on the highway and you will see cars and commercial vehicles exceeding the speed limit and following too close. Excessive speed and close following distances are the main reason for accidents on the road. It's unfortunate that this is the case when most of these accidents could have been avoided.

Other causes of accidents would include mechanical failure that would cause loss of control of the vehicle. Infrastructure failure, like a road washing out or a bridge collapse. Poor atmospheric conditions, loss of visibility because of fog, or surface ice on the road that would cause loss of control, and high winds that could cause dangerous flying debris, and even turn over trucks.

Also accidents can happen by drivers experiencing sudden health problems which are referred to as medically induced crashes, or medical emergency crashes. This can result from a variety of medical conditions such as heart attacks, strokes, seizures, diabetic episodes, or sudden loss of consciousness among others.

Some research indicates that medical emergencies are responsible for one to two percent of all traffic crashes.

So, turning our attention to excessive speed and following distance is very important for every driver. I know, this all seems well and good until you're in a hurry, or someone in front of you is going very slow, and you're not allowed to use the outside left lane.

Okay, so let's assume you just got off the phone talking to your dispatcher or customer, and they are not happy about you arriving late. You're thinking you should have got an earlier start, or not have taken that break, so now with an elevated heart rate you drive faster and follow too close to the slow vehicle in front of you. It's so common, everybody does it, they follow close to intimidate the slow car to speed up or switch lanes. Sometimes it works, right? Don't do it! Let the voice of reason speak. Excessive speed and following too closely leads to accidents, and you'll be in more hot water and quite possibly worse if you get into an accident. As one commercial driver of many years to another, I plead with you to drive safe. The best thing to do when there is a slow vehicle that you're in back of is to keep a good safe following distance and patiently wait for an opening to pass.

While commercial driver safety training tells you not to do this, while maintaining a safe following distance, sometimes I flash my headlights in an attempt to get the slow moving vehicle to move over. Take that advice with the grain of salt, but it is certainly safer than following too closely.

Let's shift our attention now to log books. If you drive more than a hundred mile radius from where you start you will be required by law to use a log. I am not going to get into all the details of log books except the most important part.

The driving school that you go to will give you a comprehensive knowledge of how to use a logbook. And the company that you choose will show you how to use their electronic log system. The main purpose of the log book is to make it so drivers are properly rested when they drive, assuring that they have proper rest periods.

Feel free to agree or disagree with me on this, but I think this is utterly absurd. This is telling me that commercial drivers are really stupid. If you didn't have the log book they would just drive until they fell asleep and go off the road and have an accident.

The log book does nothing to keep a commercial driver from driving tired, period. In my career, I have always been compliant with the hours of service regulations and often have I been too tired to drive safely.

You may be different but this is what makes me tired, driving, yes just driving can make me tired, early mornings, when it rains, excessive temperature, like in the heat of the summer or the bitter cold of winter, change of seasons, and the common cold. All these things can make me tired, and compromise safety. A stop at a rest area and a brisk walk around the vehicle will do nothing to re-energize me.

For me, there are only two things to do to keep me alert and safe to drive. The first and best thing for me to do is to pull over at a safe place and take a small nap. A ten to twenty minute nap will do wonders for me and I'll be wide awake and safe to drive. Another thing that works for me is when I have somebody to talk to.

While driving a tour bus back from a concert in Philadelphia to Maine late one night, I was very tired until one of the passengers struck up a conversation. That talk kept my mind engaged, and awake for the duration of the trip.

I have developed this mindset, and I hope for your sake and others you do too. Make it a priority above all else not to drive when you're tired. This is a fact, commercial drivers have in the past and still do on occasion fall asleep behind the wheel and cause accidents resulting in injury and death. Do what you need to do to be safe regardless of whether you arrive on time.

I plan to cover this more in the last chapter but consider this. In the US alone a significant percentage of adults lack physical activity, and thus have poor physical fitness and approximately forty percent of adults are obese. Keeping your body fit is essential for your well being and safety, and unfortunately it is often neglected.

Maintaining a safe speed is a critical factor for keeping you out of the ditch, or upside down, or worse. Almost every time without exception, while driving in the snow I see cars and trucks off the road. You really need to maintain a safe speed when you're facing slippery road conditions, and also when visibility is compromised like in the fog or at night. Turn on your four way flashers to let people know that you're going slow. If you have an outside temperature gauge, keep an eyeball on the temperature especially if it's raining. Rain can turn into dangerous freezing rain which can cause all kinds of havoc for drivers.

Obviously, the safest thing to do would be to find a safe place to park &

wait there until the conditions get better. If it's snowing maintain a larger than normal following distance, and pull over often where it's safe to clean the snow off your lights, so you'll be seen better.

One winter I was driving a day cab pulling a eight thousand gallon tanker of water on a secondary road, going up a large winding hill in the snow. The truck was doing a good job going up that hill for a while until it lost traction.

When the wheels began to spin the truck pivoted towards the ditch. With my four way flashers on I decided the best course of action was to slowly back down the hill. Having only limited success with this, and still sliding towards the ditch, I managed to stop. This in turn caused the traffic in back of me to slow down, and some got stuck, it was just a mess.

I had to wait until the road got plowed and sanded, and needed the assistance of a tow truck to pull my front wheel out of the snow bank.
One could make an argument that if I had more speed ascending up the hill that maybe I could have made it. But going off the road at a higher speed is more dangerous than going off at a slow speed.

7 DRUGS AND ALCOHOL

The world of commercial driving is tightly regulated, and for good reason. When you're behind the wheel of a multi ton vehicle, you're not just driving, you're carrying immense responsibility for the safety of everyone on the road. This is why drug and alcohol testing plays such a critical role in the industry. From pre-employment screenings to random tests, these measures aim to ensure drivers are sober, alert, and capable of performing their duties safely. But despite the seemingly rigorous framework, there are troubling inconsistencies that cast a shadow over the effectiveness of these protocols.

The process begins with pre-employment drug testing. Before a company can put you in the driver's seat, you must pass a drug test. This ensures that anyone stepping into a commercial vehicle is clean and sober at the outset of their employment. Then comes the random testing, an ongoing measure meant to keep drivers honest. These tests can happen anytime and are meant to deter substance use by the sheer unpredictability of their occurrence.

Personally, I seem to get chosen for random drug tests more frequently than most. Perhaps it's coincidence, or maybe there's some strange algorithm at work involving the first letter of my last name. Who knows? All I know is that several times a year, I'm called to report to a clinic for yet another test. While it's a minor inconvenience, I accept it as part of the job, a necessary safeguard to maintain the integrity of our profession.

However, here's where things get peculiar. If you fail a drug or alcohol test, the consequences are swift and severe. You won't get hired if it's a pre-employment screening, and if you're already employed, you'll likely be terminated upon receiving the result of a positive test. That much is clear and fair. But here's the paradox, if you show up to work reeking of marijuana, with bloodshot eyes that all but scream impairment, there's a decent chance you'll face no immediate repercussions.

It's not just my observation. I've asked the professionals who administer these tests if they ever encounter drivers who smell like marijuana, and they've confirmed it happens regularly. When I pressed further, asking whether they report such drivers to their employers, the answer was a resounding no. Their job, they explained, is strictly to administer the tests, not to police behavior. While I understand the limits of their responsibilities, this practice doesn't sit right with me. Isn't it their duty to flag potential safety risks? After all, if you're impaired behind the wheel, you're a danger to everyone.

This paradox is more than a professional curiosity, it's a public safety crisis. A driver under the influence of drugs or alcohol is a ticking time bomb on the road. Their reactions are slower, their judgment is impaired, and their ability to handle the vehicle safely is compromised. We've all seen the devastating aftermath of accidents involving commercial vehicles, jackknifed trailers, crumpled sedans, and lives irreparably shattered. Knowing some of these could be prevented makes the issue all the more infuriating.

I'm fully aware that there are a wide range of drugs out there, substances that are harder to detect, and carry no telltale smell. That makes the issue of impaired driving even more concerning, as the absence of obvious signs doesn't mean someone is safe to drive. For me, this underscores the importance of vigilance. When I do encounter something unmistakable, like the strong smell of marijuana as a driver steps out of their cab, I don't hesitate to act.

I've made it a personal policy to take action in these situations. I'll note the company name and truck number and report it to the authorities. Some might see this as overzealous, but to me, it's a moral obligation. Driving under the influence, whether it's marijuana, alcohol, or harder to detect drugs, isn't just a bad decision. It's a potential death sentence for innocent people sharing the road. The stakes are simply too high to ignore.

Agree with me or not, but this is an issue that demands attention. Drug and alcohol use has no place in commercial driving. The stakes are simply too high. As drivers, we have a responsibility not only to ourselves and our employers but also to the countless families who share the road with us. It's a responsibility I take seriously, and I believe everyone in this industry should do the same.

The current system, with its paradoxes and blind spots, is far from perfect. But with vigilance and a commitment to accountability, we can work toward a safer future, one where the risks posed by impaired drivers are minimized, and the roads are just a little bit safer for everyone.

I'll conclude this chapter with the story of the Carrollton bus collision.

On the night of May 14, 1988, a devastating accident occurred on Interstate 71 near Carrollton Kentucky, underscoring the catastrophic consequences of impaired driving. Larry Mahoney, a thirty year old factory worker, was driving his pickup truck northbound in the southbound lanes of the interstate. His blood alcohol concentration was found to be 0.24%, three times the legal limit.

At approximately 10:55 p.m., Mahoney's truck collided head on with a church bus returning from an amusement park outing. The bus, carrying 63 passengers, burst into flames upon impact due to the rupture of its unprotected fuel tank. The inferno claimed the lives of 27 individuals, many of them children, and injured thirty four others.

This tragedy stands as one of the deadliest bus accidents in U.S. history and highlights the severe repercussions of driving under the influence. In the aftermath, significant changes were implemented in vehicle safety standards and drunk driving laws to prevent such a catastrophe from recurring.

The Carrollton bus collision serves as a somber reminder of the critical importance of sobriety in commercial driving. It underscores the necessity for stringent drug and alcohol testing protocols to ensure the safety of all road users.

8 PERSONAL PRIVACY CONCERNS

When you choose a career in commercial driving, you quickly realize that privacy isn't something you can count on. Whether it's mandatory drug and alcohol testing, GPS tracking, or electronic logging devices ELDs, every aspect of your work is monitored to some degree. The justification for this is usually safety, ensuring drivers are alert, compliant, and operating within legal limits. While some of these measures make sense, recent developments are pushing the boundaries of privacy to uncomfortable extremes. For many drivers, this raises a pressing question, where is the line between ensuring safety and violating personal privacy?

One of the most controversial intrusions into driver privacy is the forward facing camera. While cameras facing the road are nothing new, the rise of inward facing cameras has sparked widespread concern. Imagine driving for hours on end, knowing a camera is pointed directly at you, recording your every move. Do you fidget too much? Look tired for a moment? Adjust the radio a little too often? All of it is being captured, potentially to be scrutinized later.

I have one of these cameras in my truck now. To be fair, it's covered, for now. The company policy is that drivers who have been with the company for a long time and are considered trustworthy get a camera with a cover. This concession feels like a nod to our seniority and experience, but let's not kid ourselves. The infrastructure is in place. If the company decided to activate those cameras tomorrow, there would be nothing we could do about it. It's not hard to see where this is heading either. New drivers aren't getting the same leniency. They're expected to accept the cameras, & over time, this will just become the norm.

It's a classic case of what I call turnkey totalitarianism. The system is built incrementally. First, they introduce the cameras and tell you, "Don't worry, they're turned off." Then, over time, they start using them selectively, maybe for new hires or as part of a pilot program. Eventually, it becomes standard practice. By the time most drivers realize what's happened, the proverbial cage has been built around them.

This incremental approach is a lot like the old story of the frog in boiling water. If you throw a frog into a pot of boiling water, it'll jump out. But if you put it in cool water and slowly heat it up, the frog doesn't notice until it's too late. That's exactly how these invasive measures creep into our lives. They don't roll out everything all at once. They start small, with just a few cameras or limited applications. Then, little by little, they expand the scope until resistance becomes futile.

Now, let me be clear, truck drivers aren't saints. We've all heard stories about drivers who cut corners, break rules, or even engage in reckless behavior. Some of these cameras were undoubtedly introduced in response to incidents where drivers were at fault. But that doesn't mean every driver should be treated as a potential criminal. Just because some people abuse the system doesn't justify the blanket surveillance of everyone in the industry.

It's not just drivers who are imperfect either. Trucking companies and dispatchers are far from flawless. Dispatchers often push drivers to the limit, in some cases, encouraging them to skirt regulations or take risks to meet tight delivery schedules. And with inward facing cameras, companies gain a powerful tool to shift blame onto drivers. Video footage can be edited, taken out of context, or selectively used to make the driver look bad. Did you glance at your phone for a second at a stoplight? Did you yawn after a long shift? That footage could be used against you, even if it didn't impact your ability to drive safely.

The introduction of inward facing cameras also shifts the power dynamics between drivers and their employers. Surveillance gives companies an unprecedented level of control over their workforce. They can monitor not just your driving habits but also your facial expressions, body language, and even your mood. This level of scrutiny can be dehumanizing, reducing drivers to mere data points in a system that prioritizes efficiency over individuality.

There's also the question of who controls the data. Once the footage is recorded, it becomes the property of the company. Who gets to see it? How long is it stored? Could it be shared with third parties, like insurance companies or law enforcement? These are important questions, and drivers rarely get clear answers. The potential for misuse is enormous, and the lack of transparency only makes it worse.

The surveillance doesn't stop with cameras. ELDs already track our every move, down to the minute. GPS systems monitor our location at all times. Some companies are even experimenting with wearable devices that track drivers' heart rates and other biometric data to assess fatigue levels. Where does it end? At what point do we say enough is enough?

To be fair, safety is a legitimate concern in this industry. Commercial vehicles are massive, and accidents can have catastrophic consequences. But safety and privacy don't have to be mutually exclusive. Companies need to strike a balance between monitoring for safety and respecting the personal space and dignity of their drivers. Forward facing cameras are a step too far. They're invasive, unnecessary, and open the door to a host of ethical and legal issues.

If companies are serious about improving safety, they should focus on solutions that address the root causes of accidents, like fatigue, unrealistic delivery schedules, and poor physical fitness. Surveillance is a shortcut that avoids dealing with these deeper issues. It's easier to point a camera at a driver than to address systemic problems in the industry.

Commercial drivers are the backbone of the economy, moving goods across the country and keeping supply chains running. We deserve respect, not constant surveillance. Privacy is a fundamental right, and it doesn't disappear just because we drive for a living. If we allow these invasive measures to become normalized, we're setting a dangerous precedent, not just for our industry but for society as a whole.

It's time for drivers to stand up and demand better. We need clear policies that protect our privacy while ensuring safety on the roads. We need companies that value their drivers as people, not just as data points. And most importantly, we need to push back against the creeping normalization of surveillance before it's too late. The water is heating up, let's not be the frog.

9 WHERE'S THE BATHROOM?

It goes without saying that humans need bathrooms. This isn't some revolutionary observation, it's a basic fact of life. But for truck drivers, one of the most essential human functions has become a frustrating and often humiliating challenge. You'd think that the people who deliver the products that keep this country running would have a modicum of respect and access to basic facilities. Yet more and more, truck drivers are being denied access to clean, usable bathrooms.

The problem has gotten worse in recent years, particularly since COVID-19 upended normal routines. Before the pandemic, many shippers and receivers allowed truck drivers to use their facilities, and while some were less than pristine, they were at least functional. But COVID created a new level of paranoia, with many businesses locking their doors to drivers entirely under the guise of "health and safety."

This meant that while truck drivers were still delivering food, medicine, and other essential goods during the height of the pandemic, and keeping the economy afloat, they were being denied access to something as simple as a toilet. Now, even as the world has largely moved on from pandemic restrictions, many of these businesses haven't reinstated restroom access for drivers.

For some facilities, the "solution" has been to install porta potties outside for drivers. But let's be honest, no one wants to make a bowel movement in a porta potty, especially one that's been sitting in the sun all day, often without regular cleaning or access to running water for handwashing. It's unsanitary and degrading, and it sends a clear message, "We don't really care about your comfort or dignity."

Sure, truck drivers are mostly men, and for urination, they can often make do in ways that don't require a bathroom. But for anything else, the lack of proper facilities becomes a serious issue. The idea that a worker who spends ten to sixteen hours a day on the road can't count on finding a clean bathroom is absurd.

The lack of accessible bathrooms has forced many drivers to improvise. A common, though deeply unpleasant solution, is to carry a five gallon bucket lined with a plastic bag, along with a supply of kitty litter. When faced with no other option, this makeshift toilet can serve in emergencies. Drivers can't always count on a truck stop or rest area to be nearby, and when nature calls, it doesn't wait.

While this method is practical in a pinch, it's far from ideal. Using a bucket in the cramped space of a truck cab is degrading and unsanitary, and disposing of the waste responsibly adds another layer of hassle. That so many drivers have been forced to resort to this speaks volumes about the broken state of the industry.

This issue cuts to the heart of a larger problem, the disconnect between what people say about truck drivers and how they treat them. People claim to "appreciate truck drivers" and recognize their vital role in the economy, but actions speak louder than words. If businesses truly valued truck drivers, they wouldn't make it so difficult for them to access something as basic as a restroom.

That said, truck drivers aren't without fault in this situation. In talking to shippers and receivers, I've heard some unsettling stories. Drivers flushing paper towels down the toilet, causing costly plumbing problems. Others trimming their beards in the bathroom and leaving the sink littered with hair. I can understand why this would frustrate a business owner or employee, no one wants to clean up someone else's mess.

But here's the problem, by behaving this way, these drivers are shooting themselves in the foot. They're giving businesses a reason to deny bathroom access to all drivers, creating a collective punishment for what is ultimately the fault of a few bad apples. The result is that the vast majority of drivers, who are respectful and responsible, are paying the price for the actions of a small minority.

The life of a truck driver is hard enough as it is. The long hours, the isolation, and the physical toll of the job are challenges that most people don't understand. Add to that the difficulty of navigating a massive truck and trailer into parking lots that weren't designed to accommodate them. Many places where drivers might be able to find a bathroom simply aren't an option because there's no room for the truck to turn around or park.

Truck stops and rest areas can help fill the gap, but they're not always conveniently located or open when you need them. And for drivers who are on tight schedules or trying to avoid violating hours of service regulations, taking a detour to find a bathroom isn't always feasible.

So what's the solution? For starters, businesses need to reconsider their policies. Denying bathroom access to the very people who are delivering their products is not only disrespectful but counterproductive. Businesses that value their relationships with drivers, and by extension, their supply chains, should ensure that clean, functional restrooms are available.

Drivers too, have a role to play. Those who are causing problems in restrooms need to recognize that their actions affect the entire community. By treating facilities with respect, they can help rebuild trust and improve access for everyone.

On a larger scale, the trucking industry needs to advocate for better conditions for drivers, including restroom access. This is already happening in some states, Washington passed a law in 2022 mandating bathroom access for truck drivers, but more widespread action is needed.

The lack of bathroom access for truck drivers is more than an inconvenience, it's a sign of a deeper problem in how society values the people who keep it running. Truck drivers deserve better, not just because they're essential workers, but because they're human beings. Ensuring access to clean functional restrooms is a small but meaningful step toward showing them the respect they deserve.

This is about more than bathrooms. It's about recognizing the dignity and humanity of the people who make modern life possible. The sight of a five gallon bucket and kitty litter in the back of a truck cab should be a call to action, not a permanent solution. Let's start treating truck drivers with the appreciation and respect they've more than earned.

10 ALL THINGS CONSIDERED

In this chapter we're going to go over the pros and cons of being a commercial driver.

It's essential that you look ahead and think about these things before considering a career behind the wheel. The romance of the open road has long been a compelling force, drawing many into the career of commercial truck or bus driving. There's something undeniably liberating about the hum of the engine, and the ever changing landscape that unfolds mile after mile.

For those who revel in solitude and the thrill of new locales, commercial driving can seem like a dream come true. One of the most significant advantages of a career in commercial driving is the sense of freedom it offers. Unlike traditional nine to five jobs, drivers are often their own bosses on the road, especially long haul truckers who may not see their actual boss for weeks at a time. This autonomy allows drivers to enjoy the landscape, listen to their favorite podcast or music, and experience a sense of Independence that is hard to find in other professions.

Flexibility can also be a perk, particularly for truck and bus drivers on local or regional Routes who can enjoy consistent routes with the ability to return home at the end of the day.

Commercial driving is also a career that comes with a level of economic stability. The demand for drivers is consistent and growing, thanks to the ever increasing needs of both the freight and transportation sectors. With the right certifications, such as those for hazardous materials, drivers can significantly increase their earnings. Furthermore, the advent of e-commerce has only boosted the need for delivery drivers, ensuring that the truck driving profession remains lucrative.

However, this career is not without its cons, and they weigh heavily on the scale. Perhaps the most significant of these is the impact on personal relationships. Being away from home for days, weeks, or even months, can strain even the strongest relationships. Family events, anniversaries, and some of life's small moments tend to happen without the driver around, which can lead to feelings of isolation and guilt. For those with family members who have special needs, the challenges are even more pronounced. Regular care, attendance at therapy sessions, and simply being present for emotional support are critical needs that can't always be met from the road. Managing these responsibilities from a distance can be stressful, and the physical absence of a truck or bus driver can place an additional burden on their partners or other family members.

Property care is another practical concern. A home left unattended due to frequent travels can fall into disrepair. Seasonal concerns such as lawn care, snow removal, and general maintenance can become logistical nightmares. This job takes a toll on one's physical and mental health as well. Long hours seated in a confined space can lead to back problems, obesity, and other health issues. The solitude, while peaceful at times, can morph into profound loneliness and depression. The monotony of the road can also lead to a mental fog, which truckers often refer to humorously as "white line fever", where the endless white lines of the road hypnotize one into a state of mental autopilot.

Interestingly, the road also offers time for reflection and self discovery. Between the endless miles, drivers meet a variety of people and experience the multifaceted cultural tapestry of the country in a way few other professions offer. Each state line crossed is a new chapter, and each roadside diner is a chance to meet new people. It's these slices of Americana that often bring a smile to the weary driver's face.

Choosing a career as a commercial truck or bus driver is akin to choosing a lifestyle. For many, the benefits of good pay, independence, and the open road are enough to outweigh the downsides. But for others, the sacrifices, especially the time away from loved ones and the physical toll, maybe too great in the end. Like any road worth traveling, it's filled with unexpected bumps and beautiful vistas. The key is knowing what you value most and whether you're ready for the long haul, both literally and metaphorically.

In my personal experience, after driving for over 30 years, I understand the longing to do something else. The open road has its charm, but it's not uncommon to reach a point where you consider other paths. However, what's truly fascinating is that some people, even those in the professional world, doctors, lawyers, CEOs, and others, choose to take an entirely different route later in life, leaving their prestigious careers behind to pursue long haul trucking. It might seem like an unusual leap, but for many, it's a conscious decision born from a mix of practicality, passion, and a desire for freedom.

Take for example, the story of Dr. John McElligott, a former physician who decided to embrace the trucking life after decades in the medical field. McElligott initially became involved with trucking by providing medical care to truck drivers, but over time, he grew fascinated with the lifestyle. When he retired from practicing medicine, he decided to hit the road himself, finding solace and a sense of purpose in long haul trucking. His background in medicine also gave him a unique perspective, as he became an advocate for drivers' health, blending his two worlds in a way that benefited others.

Then there's the case of Peter Armstrong, a corporate executive who spent years working in finance before trading his corner office for the cab of an 18 wheeler. Burned out from the relentless pace and stress of the corporate world, Armstrong sought a simpler, more grounded life. He found trucking appealing because it offered independence, the chance to see the country, and the satisfaction of a job well done. His story reflects the sentiment of many professionals who tire of office politics and rigid schedules, longing for the freedom that comes with the open road.

Another example is Susan Turner, a former lawyer who had spent decades litigating in courtrooms and working grueling hours in a high stakes environment. After retiring from her law practice, Turner decided she wasn't ready to settle into a quiet life just yet. Inspired by a friend who was a truck driver, she decided to pursue her CDL and start a second career in long haul trucking. Turner often says that trucking gives her the sense of adventure and purpose she craved, without the stress of legal deadlines or courtroom battles.

Perhaps the most unexpected transition is that of Robert Winslow, a retired software engineer who spent his career developing complex systems for Silicon Valley tech companies. Winslow had always loved driving and considered himself a bit of a road trip enthusiast. When he retired, he realized that trucking offered the perfect combination of work and leisure. He now spends his days driving cross country, using his technical expertise to optimize his routes and expenses while enjoying the simplicity of life on the road.

For many of these professionals, trucking isn't just a job, it's a lifestyle choice. They're drawn to the idea of independence, the chance to explore the country, and the sense of accomplishment that comes from delivering essential goods. For others, it's a financial decision. After years in professions where retirement savings may not have panned out as planned, trucking provides a way to earn a stable income while still enjoying a flexible schedule.

There's also a sense of fulfillment that many find in trucking that their previous careers didn't provide. Driving offers a tangible immediate result, you deliver a load, and you know you've contributed to keeping the economy moving. This is a stark contrast to the abstract or delayed rewards of many white collar professions.

Interestingly, there are support networks and resources tailored to help professionals make this transition. Programs like the Owner Operator Independent Drivers Association OOIDA, provide training and resources for those new to the industry, while CDL schools across the country often report an increase in retirees from other fields seeking to join the trucking workforce.

In the end, these stories prove that trucking isn't just for one type of person. The industry is as diverse as the roads it travels, welcoming people from all walks of life who are looking for something different. Whether it's the desire for freedom, the call of the open road, or simply a change of pace, trucking has become an unexpected but rewarding second act for many professionals.

Let's talk for a minute here about labor unions. Some commercial driving jobs are unionized. Even though these jobs normally pay more and offer a better benefit package, I've come to not like unions on principal. Feel free to agree or disagree with me if you want but this is my book and you're going to get my opinion. Please allow me to explain.

Labor unions, once the valiant champions of the working man, have sadly morphed into quite the paradox. Today, they come across less like defenders of the common worker and more like heavy handed enforcers of a bloated left wing agenda. It's as though they have traded their capes in for brass knuckles. In their heyday unions were bastions of solidarity and fairness, ensuring that the sweat of a man's brow earned him a fair day's pay and humane working conditions. Fast forward to now, and it appears their more interested in flexing their political muscle and padding their pockets. They've become bullies on the block, pushing around not just corporations, but anyone who dares to question their increasingly radical playbook. It's a real shame to see such a noble cause get lost in the sauce of greed and power politics.

In my time driving truck and tour bus I've had runnins with union members, here's two examples.

While delivering lumber to a building materials supply outfit near Pittsburgh Pennsylvania there were union members at the front entrance with picket signs. They were acting like terrible human beings, using bad language and calling me a scab as I drove in. When I talked to the person who unloaded my trailer, he said yeah, these guys have been a nightmare, including vandalizing their property by slashing tires on their trucks, and they sliced up the material on a soft sided flatbed trailer.

I thought to myself, if this was my company and the dispute got settled, then I'd have to hire the same guys back? Does working for a union automatically turn you into a jackass and a vandal? This makes no sense to me.

Another time, I was driving tour bus in Boston shuttling people from a trade show to a large motel, the reason I was there was because Peter Pan bus company was on strike. They were people there that each end of the route with picket signs calling me a scab and using bad language.

One guy, even got on my bus and was telling my passengers that I didn't know how to drive and just trying to make me angry, which he succeeded. If I was working for a union I would never act like that.

As of the time of writing this book the longshormen on the east coast of the United States just started striking. These people are responsible for loading and unloading container ships at the ports.

If this keeps up the supply chain is going to be negatively affected and this will create some serious problems for this country.

It's important to note that many of these people already make over six figures a year and they want more money. They also want to ban the implementation of automation equipment at the ports. They surmise that their jobs will be replaced by automation and they don't want that.

In the book, Basic Economics by Thomas Sowell, he talks about among other things a personal economy and a national economy. Imagine back when the motor car became popular, and how that put a lot of businesses that made saddles and other equipment for horse riding obsolete, and therefore they went out of business. Automation at a shipping ports would be more efficient and cost effective and result in lower cost of goods for the consumer.

 I believe that the needs of the many outweigh the needs of the few in this case. These people would just have to get new jobs. And that's all I got to say about that here.

 So, if you ever find yourself contemplating a career shift, perhaps consider this, the road is long, and maps have their limits, but sometime the journey itself is where you find what you've been looking for. After all, every mile covered is a new story to tell, and who doesn't like a good story?

11 | Body Mind and Spirit

In this last chapter I want to cover some things that are important your personal development and your general well being. Many of the things that will be covered here are things that I wish that I would have taken into consideration when I got into this career. We'll start off with the importance of taking care of your body.

An "ill" maintained body will affect your safety, your mood, and your productivity.

My advice to you is to look around at other drivers and seriously consider if you would like to be like them. Realizing the fact that some things that affect our health and well being cannot be changed but most things can. I'm thinking of the driver who is excessively overweight with a butt hanging out of his mouth and walking with a limp. This guy most likely has a very poor diet, gets little to no exercise, and is needlessly taking in dangerous tars and chemicals from smoking. The deterioration of his hips and his knees because his excessive weight causes pain which in turn affects his sleep. This guy is like a walking time bomb. Can you say, high blood pressure, stroke, heart attack? Let's call this a bad health snowball effect.

It's very common for people in this industry to ignore their health. I seen many drivers that would fit this description. It would scare you if you knew how many people like this were on the road that you share. Sure, I didn't say it was easy to work sixty or seventy hours a week and exercise and eat right.

I know, I've heard it before, "I don't have time to exercise and eat right, I need to make money". Well, news flash, you can't make money when you're dead.

To be honest, I haven't been the picture of health either for most of my driving career. But you know what? I've come a long way since being almost a hundred pounds overweight. You'd be wise to seriously consider some of the things I share here that have helped me. Because they can also help you.

I got on a campaign to keep my expenses down. The less bills I have means the less hours I need to work. I can now devote some of this time to physical fitness and preparing healthy meals.

One of the biggest wastes of money in my opinion is having a new vehicle. The prices they are getting for new vehicles these days is outrageous and they don't last any longer. I don't want a big car payment and a big full coverage insurance payment. Also I don't like the idea of supporting union thugs either.

Oh, but you say, I need something reliable. Yeah, the only thing that is really reliable about a new car is the big payment every month. I can count on one hand through the years how many times my old cars have let me down. I like to have two used vehicles, one small car and one truck so I can pull a trailer and get building materials for my house or whatever. Also when one of my vehicles has a problem I can just use the other one, and I don't need expensive full coverage insurance either.

But realizing the fact that you may also enjoy the status of having a new vehicle, kind of cool huh? Some people's priorities are as well thought out as a toddler's finger painting. There exists a curious breed of individuals who treat their cars like royalty while their own bodies languish in peasant like neglect. Picture this, a gleaming, polished masterpiece of automotive engineering, and from this dazzling Chariot steps out its lord, a person whose idea of a balanced diet is choosing weather or not to supersize their meal before rolling up to the drive thru window. It's an ironic spectacle to me. There they are, the proud car owner, puffing and panting just from the herculean effort of exiting their mobile throne. The car, with it's pristine paint job and horsepower enough to launch it into orbit, stands in stark contrast to its driver, who's most strenuous cardio session likely includes reaching for a TV remote or a distant bag of potato chips.

Seriously now, let's go over some things that have helped me. The Bible says, as a man thinks so is he. The first and most important thing we need to do is to change our thinking, this will in turn change our behavior.

The internet is loaded with videos and podcasts about health and fitness. Start watching and listening to them even if you don't feel like it. Learn all about vitamins. Did you know that there are good vitamins and some that are just trash? Do your research. Watch the videos about vegetable and seed oils. Watch videos by Dr. Berg and Dr. Ken Berry. Do not think it's going to take just one evening of watching these videos. Try to take in one or more of these videos every week. When you do this you will learn a great deal about nutrition and about the very unhealthy ingredients that's in processed food. You will also learn the right nutritional products for you to buy. You'll learn about different exercising routines that will be good for you and more. There is much to learn about beyond the scope of this book.

The following is a list of what I've been doing as far as nutrition and exercise. Although this is working for me don't just take my word for it, you need to do your own research. I have been doing the carnivore diet. But not strict carnivore, you could call it a mostly meat diet. Dr. Ken Berry does a great job in his videos discussing the many benefits of the carnivore diet and the how tos.

I eat mostly beef but I also eat some cheese, milk, eggs, and a little Korean kimchi.

I know, you was told that red meat is not good for you. I don't know about you but do you trust the government? It seems like the right thing to do is often the opposite of what the government says. .

Normally I eat until I am comfortably stuffed. This is a nutrient dense diet therefore it's easier to fast. I do intermittent fasting most days for at least

17 hours, the most I have gone is 3 days. Also I try to avoid any vegetable or seed oils, sugars, breads, rice, and carbs in general. I've been taking one day a week for a cheat meal where I eat whatever I want. I have also been limiting my alcohol consumption to that one day a week and obviously going light on the alcohol.

The supplements I've been taking include creatine monohydrate, vitamin B12, vitamin D3 and K2, a half of an aspirin, CoQ10, magnesium citrate, cod liver oil, krill oil, and nattokinase. My exercise routine consists of some weight lifting, and rucking, which is walking with weights in a backpack. This has helped me tremendously and I highly recommend it. My plan is to continue my research and refine my diet and exercise routine accordingly.

My final recommendation on this topic is to learn as much as you can, watch videos, read books, and take action to preserve your health.

Now let's focus on the mind. "Intellectual growth should commence at birth and cease only at death." Albert Einstein.

As a commercial driver you have a great opportunity to take in information for your intellectual growth. All you need is your phone, your vehicles radio, Bluetooth speaker, and or an earpiece.

Find yourself news sources you can trust and learn as much as you can about what's going on in your country and your world, and hopefully this will lead you to participate in the political process to help bring about the betterment of mankind.

I've been listening to Glenn Beck for years now and other commentators on his platform, Blaze Media. I believe Glenn really cares about people and is a true patriot. He is a hero to me in that respect.

"All that's needed for evil to triumph is for good men to do nothing." Edmond Burke". You would probably agree with me that there's a lot a bad stuff going on in our country and around the world.

We have an infiltration of Marxism in our public schools, higher learning institutions, and our government. Also the radical left is sexualizing our kids in our public schools. Not to mention out of control government spending and open border policies that are destroying this country.

I talk a lot more about this subject on my video episodes Symposium On The Sea. But for now I'll be brief on this subject and stop here.

You can literally get an education from behind the wheel. The possibilities are endless, really. I wish I would have started listening to audiobooks early in my driving career but I didn't. I'd listen to mostly music and some mindless stuff like Art Bell for instance.

Seems like wherever I was in the country I could surf the AM dial late at night I would come across Coast to Coast with Art Bell. Art Bell was the ringmaster of the absurd. Each night offered a buffet of the bizarre, like crop circles, conspiracy theories, interdimensional beings, time travelers, and of course UFOs and aliens. I guess listening to this once in awhile to keep one awake is ok but a steady diet of it is certainly no good.

Often the way I find good books is from recommendations in other books, videos, or podcasts. If I'm interested in the subject matter I write the title down in a notebook to buy later.

So moving on, we covered the body, the mind, now let's conclude this chapter by talking about our spirit.

"Come to me, all who labor and are heavy laden, and I will give you rest. Take my yoke upon you, and learn of me, for I am gentle and lowly in heart, and you will find rest for your souls." Matthew 11:28

Many of us know people who seem to be quite emotionally stable and lead fulfilling lives without claiming to have any religious beliefs. My purpose is not to argue this point here.

The bible says God is the source of true peace. The peace, hope, joy, and sense of purpose that I experience in my life, does come directly from my faith in God and my understanding of the Bible. This hasn't always been the case in my life, and it's been a process.

My dad had a strong faith in the Lord and it was evident in how he lived his life. My father was not one for using bad language or skipping church, and he prayed often. Perhaps even a stronger evidence of his faith would be how he conducted his business dealings and how he helped and cared for people.

The bible says, if you have faith without works then your faith is dead. As far back as I can remember I believed in God. I understand now it was more of an intellectual belief, like I believe George Washington was the first president. Just believing in God is different than having a real faith in him. I'll put it this way, if I was accused of being a Christian, I don't believe they would find enough evidence for a conviction. The bible says that God has dealt every man a measure of faith. Whether we choose to accept him or reject him is up to us.

Me and my family went to a catholic church when I was growing up. There are many notable differences between going to a catholic church and let's say a baptist church for instance. I will not get into all the differences here except to say, you don't normally bring a bible when you go to a catholic church.

So there I was, my trailer doors open and backed up to a dock at the Hunt's ketchup plant in Pittsburgh Pennsylvania. I proceeded in the building to sweep out my trailer before they loaded it. A man on a forklift greeted me and took my pickup number for the load I was supposed to get. I watched as he quickly zoomed back and forth with breakneck speed loading my truck with two pallets of product at a time. When he was done loading my truck he turned off his forklift and came up to me and said, "do you know where you're going to go when you die?"

I didn't expect that. Looking back on it now that guy must have had a serious faith, and some guts. Bewildered at the question, I said, "I hope I'm going to heaven? He told me that the bible says that you can know if you're going to heaven and then he asked if he could pray with me. Feeling a little bit strange and on the spot I said, "sure." The prayer went something like this.

 Father God I realize that I'm a sinner and I believe that you sent your only son Jesus to die on a cross to forgive my sins. Please save my soul and help me turn away from my sin and follow you. I ask this in the name of the Lord Jesus Christ, Amen.

Shortly after the prayer I was headed out to my truck with my paperwork in hand off to my next destination.

To tell you the truth, I didn't feel any burden lifted off my soul after that prayer or any otherwise supernatural experience. Going along to get along was probably what I was thinking more during the prayer than being burdened over my sin.

But ironically, or perhaps not, soon after that I discovered bible teaching on the radio and I listened intently. Before this, I knew little to nothing of what the bible had to say. I'd listen to preachers like Chuck Swindoll, John MacArthur, Charles Stanley, and David Jeremiah, to mention a few.

Then naturally I had to get a bible and read it for myself. Then I decided when I go home I'm going to look for a church that teaches the bible and start going.

The key word, "saved" meaning literally, saved from an eternity in Hell. The Bible directly says how to be saved and how to know that you are saved. The biggest thing that puzzled me is that we didn't hear that when I was a kid going to catholic church. This is the most important part, right?

In conclusion I will say this, I now have a biblical worldview. I believe and understand that all of creation is a deliberate and intricate work by God, as described in the book of genesis. The bible tells us that in the beginning,

God created the heavens and the Earth. Affirming that everything from the smallest atom to the vast expanse of the universe is the handy work of the divine creator. God ingenuously designed laws such as gravity, which not only govern physical movement but also reflect his nature of order and consistency. Just as the existence of gravity is an observable and undeniable fact in the physical realm, so too is the presence of God's hand in the complexity and order of nature and a testament to his reality and sovereignty in the spiritual realm. Every sunrise, the diversity of life, and the intricate balance of the ecosystems are seen as daily reminders and manifestations of his creativity, power, an ongoing relationship with his creation.

No matter who you are or what you have done you can also experience the forgiveness and restoration of the Lord. Call out to him today.

Thank you for reading this book, and I hope you have a great future.

MY OTHER BOOKS

#1

TOP NEW

RELEASE

ON AMAZON

SCAN ME & BUY NOW

MY OTHER BOOKS

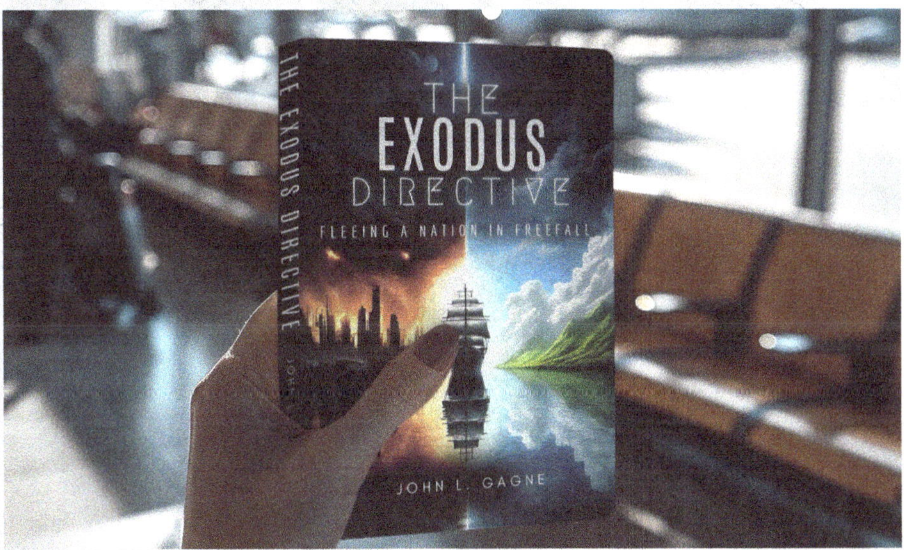

SCAN ME & BUY NOW

THE END